Of Mythic Wo
Works from th
Distant Past through
the Present

Drawing Papers 151

Participating Artists

Jo Baer
Roland Barthes
Jordan Belson
Robert Bittenbender
Lee Bontecou
Cameron
Barbara Chase-Riboud
Mel Chin
Walter De Maria
Ilka Gedő
Morris Graves
Hu Zhengyan
Steffani Jemison
Arnold J. Kemp
Mohammed O. Khalil
Duane Linklater
Janet Malcolm
Yutaka Matsuzawa
Elizabeth Milleker
Georgia O'Keeffe
I. Rice Pereira
Julia Phillips
Betye Saar
Andrei Tarkovsky
Lenore Tawney
Warlimpirrnga Tjapaltjarri
Bernadette Van-Huy
Jack Whitten
Cici Wu

The Drawing Center

Of Mythic Worlds: Works from the Distant Past through the Present

Olivia Shao

With contributors
Elise Duryee-Browner
E. C. Feiss
Maya Hayda
Annie Ochmanek
Lauren O’Neill-Butler

Contents

Director's Foreword

Laura Hoptman

The Drawing Center has a well-documented history of giving platform to an enormously broad range of artists whose visions shape the way we look at the world. Lesser known is our institution's role in creating opportunities for the New York art community to experience the creativity of curators with extraordinary expertise and/or compelling views on culture and its role in our lives. For nearly fifty years, The Drawing Center has hosted exhibitions organized by curators, artists, art historians, and experts in fields ranging from fine art to tattoos, all in a quest to present drawing at its most contemporary and provocative. In the spirit of this tradition, The Drawing Center thanks Olivia Shao, the guest curator for *Of Mythic Worlds*, for bringing her singular vision to our galleries. We invited Shao, an independent curator based in New York and, periodically, Hong Kong, to curate a show not because we had a specific exhibition in mind but because we wanted to give this interesting and unique independent curatorial voice the opportunity to tell her truths through the lens of drawing. What she has come up with is a visual essay composed of approximately fifty works on paper by creators ranging from a Qing dynasty calligrapher to the contemporary artist Julia Phillips. The presentation includes works by artists like Georgia O'Keeffe and Jack Whitten, writers like Roland Barthes and Janet Malcolm, and even the filmmaker Andrei Tarkovsky.

Each of the drawings in *Of Mythic Worlds* reflects its unique history, but each is also an expression of what Shao describes as a "universal pursuit to understand that which is outside of our objective, worldly experience." Some works are spiritual in nature; others, outright religious. Still others are reflective of esoteric, even occult belief systems. All, though, describe their relationship to the inchoate with a wordless pictorialism, whether abstractly or symbolically.

Of Mythic Worlds maps a universe of belief systems connected and diverse at the same time. Though there is a narrative to the show, it turns out to be less of a tale and more of a visual picture of an attitude towards the art object. In this exhibition, works on paper have magical associations; they are portals to other dimensions–mental, spiritual, psycho-geographical, and otherwise. Arranged around the gallery as individual entities, the space surrounding each artwork gives them a precious, almost sacred quality. In these works, all marks are mandalas and all mandalas are abstract drawings. For a small exhibition, *Of Mythic Worlds* tackles enormous ideas and travels in time across a vast art historical and geographic landscape. It is a contemporary exhibition not only because it includes some works that have been created in the past five years but because its theme of searching for existential meaning–that which lies beyond our verbal capacity to describe it–is something that all of us have experienced in these challenging times.

The Drawing Center is grateful to Olivia Shao for bringing this provocative and beautiful show and its accompanying publication to The Drawing Center. Institutional and private lenders are thanked separately by the curator, but The Drawing Center reiterates its gratitude for the collegiality of lending institutions like The Museum of Modern Art, the Centre Pompidou, the Georgia O'Keeffe Museum, the Yale University Art Gallery, and the Shaker Museum in Chatham and New Lebanon, New York.

Lead financial support for *Of Mythic Worlds* has been provided by the Burger Collection, Hong Kong, and the TOY family, along with The Andy Warhol Foundation for the Visual Arts. Generous funding is provided by the ADAA Foundation, the Fundación Almine y Bernard Ruiz-Picasso para el Art, Lonti Ebers, and Gagosian. Additional support is provided by The Director's Circle of The Drawing Center. We are grateful to all of these funders as their visions are ambitious, challenging, compassionate, and in every way equal to that of Olivia Shao, our extraordinary guest curator.

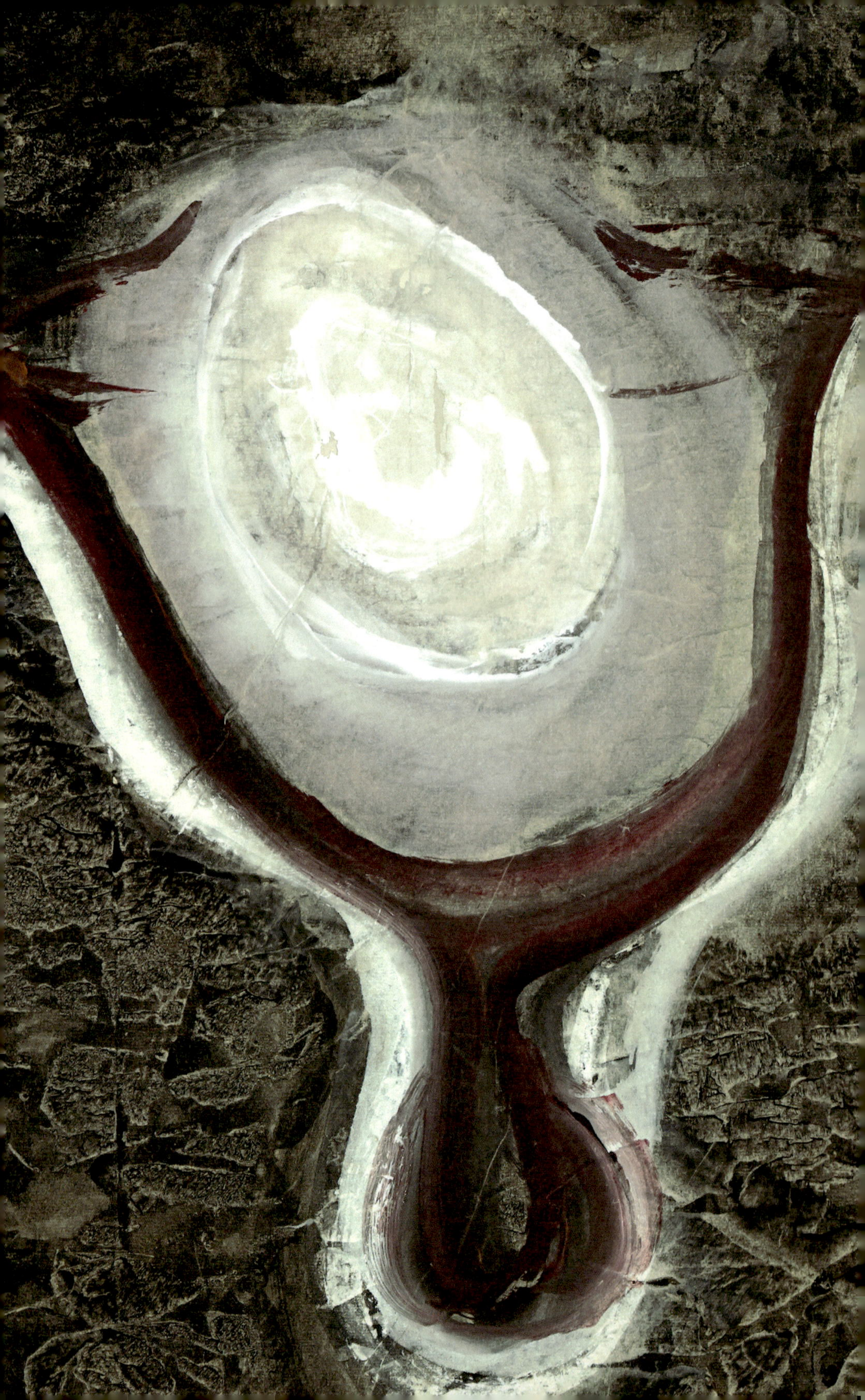

Acknowledgments

Olivia Shao

When Laura Hoptman invited me to organize an exhibition in 2019, I was more than thrilled to have the opportunity to work with The Drawing Center, an institution that I have admired for many years. Drawings and works on paper are one of my favorite mediums; they can be viewed as a direct transmission from the brain to the hand and the purest germination of an idea. I am extremely grateful to Laura for this incredible invitation, for her belief and support, and for the curatorial freedom she has given me. It has been a pleasure working with the amazing team at The Drawing Center to see this exhibition come to fruition.

I would like to extend my deepest appreciation to all the artists and lenders for their participation in the exhibition. Thank you to Jo Baer for taking part in this exhibition and to Renee Brown, Samanthe Rubell, Simone Shields, and Jessica Lally from Pace Gallery for making it possible to show Jo's exquisite drawings. Sincerest thanks to Raymond Foye for extending time, effort, and generosity; in addition, thank you to Catherine Heinrich and to Ted Turner at Matthew Marks for arranging the Jordan Belson loans. My thanks to Robert Bittenbender and to Matt Keegan for graciously lending work. Thanks also to Nicole Klagsbrun and The Cameron Parsons Foundation for lending works. Thank you to Mel Chin for the wonderful exchanges and Amanda Wiles for lending Mel's incredible drawing. Thanks to Elizabeth and Michael Childress from the Walter De Maria estate for time and dedication, and to Eva Wildes and the team at Gagosian for assistance with the loan. A special thank you to David Wojciechowski at Shepherd Gallery for very kindly introducing me to Ilka Gedő's work. Thank you to halley k harrisburg and Michael Rosenfeld for lending from your personal collection and to the team at Michael Rosenfeld Gallery for your help with the loan and image rights. My thanks to Steffani Jemison; to Carol Greene and Kai Matsumiya for giving support and insight; to Candace Barasch for generously lending from her collection; to Lisa Schiff and team for arranging the loan; and a special thanks to Taylor Walsh at Greene Naftali. Thank you to Arnold J. Kemp for our conversations and for being a part of this exhibition; thanks also to Jose Martos and the team at Martos gallery for lending the work. My thanks to Mohammed O. Khalil for contributing to this exhibition and for sharing wisdom and friendship all these years. Thanks to Duane Linklater for many wonderful conversations and for making work especially for this exhibition; and to Catriona Jeffries for facilitating the loans. Many thanks to Anne Malcolm for your generosity in lending Janet Malcolm's works, and further thanks to Lori Bookstein and Joseph Bunge for your assistance with Malcolm's work. A special thanks to Reiko Tomii and the Matsuzawa Family for your expertise and knowledge; and many, many thanks to Stephen Cheng, Alex Lau, Ching Ching Cheung, and the team at Empty Gallery for your kindness, support, and help with Matsuzawa's loan. Thank you to Elizabeth Milleker for being a part of this exhibition. It has been wonderful getting to know you. Thanks also to Anita Shapolsky for generously lending the I. Rice Pereira drawing. Thank you to Julia Phillips, and additional thanks to Beau Rutland at Matthew Marks for all of your help. A special thank you to Ales Ortuzar, Alex Worcester, and the team at Ortuzar Projects for your support, generosity, and for making it possible to show the incredible Betye Saar work; thank you also to the private collector who generously lent the work. Thank you to Clay Hapaz and Irfan Brkovic for compiling film clips and to the Andrei Tarkovsky estate. Thanks also to Kathleen Mangan at the Lenore Tawney Foundation; and to Hannah Robinson and team at Alison Jacques Gallery for your time and assistance with the loan. My thanks to Warlimpirrnga Tjapaltjarri and to Alissa Friedman at Salon 94 for your knowledge, insight, and enthusiasm; it has been a pleasure working with you to land the perfect piece. Thanks to Steve Martin and Anne Stringfield for lending to this exhibition. Thank you to Bernadette Van-Huy; to Thea Westreich Wagner and Ethan Wagner for kindly lending; and to John Burkhart for lending and help with images. Thanks to the Jack Whitten Estate, Yuta Nakajima, and the knowledgeable team at Hauser and Wirth. Thank you to Cici Wu for our several Zoom calls discussing your work; to Olivia Rubell and team for granting our loan request and helping with administration;

and to Jasmine at 47 Canal for connecting us. Many thanks to Joost van den Bergh for your graciousness and knowledge, and for lending to the exhibition.

I am grateful to the institutions that generously lent works to this exhibition. Thank you to Christophe Cherix at The Museum of Modern Art, and additional thanks to Emily Cushman for your help with the loans and framing. Thank you to the Centre Pompidou for lending the incredible Roland Barthes works and thanks to the Georgia O'Keeffe Museum and Georgia O'Keeffe Foundation for making it possible to include several beautiful drawings. Thank you to the Yale University Art Gallery for lending the powerful Barbara Chase-Riboud work on paper from their collection. Thank you also to Penn Museum, especially Allison McLaughlin for facilitating the loans and Zac Dell'Orto for advice and help with framing. My thanks to Jerry Grant for sharing extensive knowledge and to the Shaker Museum in New York. Thank you as well to MoMA PS1 for coordinating the loan of Mel Chin's work.

Many thanks to the contributors who wrote for this publication: Phillippa Shao, Lauren O'Neill-Butler, Annie Ochmanek, Elise Duryee-Browner, E. C. Feiss, and Maya Hayda. Your insights are invaluable. A special thanks to Anne Malcolm and Marta Werner for allowing us to reprint the conversation between Werner and Janet Malcolm.

My deepest gratitude to the wonderful team at The Drawing Center: Laura Hoptman, Olga Valle Tetkowski, Rebecca Brickman, Rebecca DiGiovanna, Aimee Good, and Allison Underwood for guidance, advice, and keeping us on schedule; Joanna Ahlberg and Peter Ahlberg for your expertise in making this book; Kate Robinson for your invaluable assistance with all of the loans and details; Isabella Kapur for all of your support and help; and Aaron Zimmerman and team for your efforts towards the installation.

A special thanks to Alexander Gorlizki for sharing deep insight, kindness, and generosity.

Thank you to the friends whose conversations and insights helped shaped this exhibition: especially to Phillippa Shao for all of your help and our ongoing dialogue, Richard Aldrich, Nick Hochstetler, Matthew Langan-Peck, Barbara Moore, Annie Ochmanek, Lauren O'Neill-Butler, Tony Oursler, and Jay Sanders.

A final thanks to anyone who I may have unintentionally forgotten. This exhibition involved the efforts of so many over the course of several years. I am grateful to all who assisted and contributed along the way.

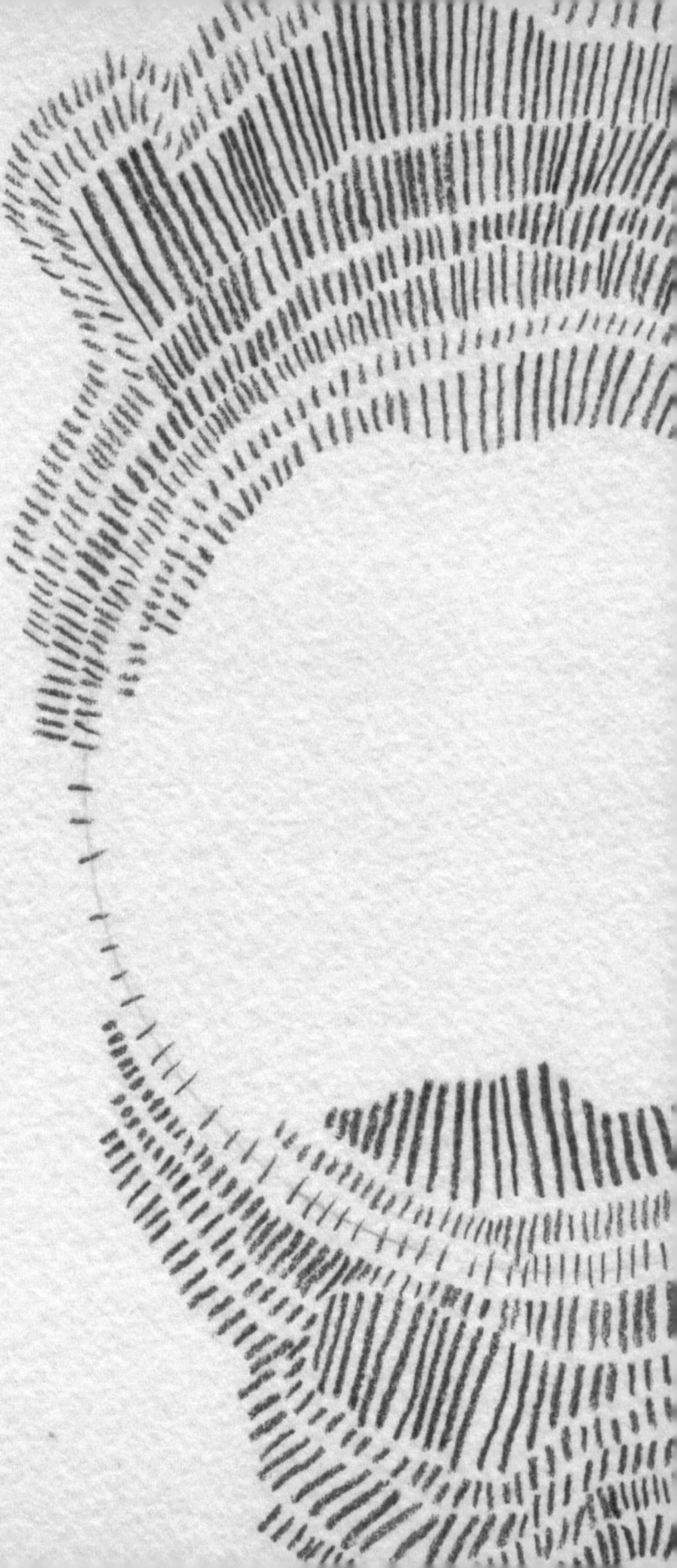

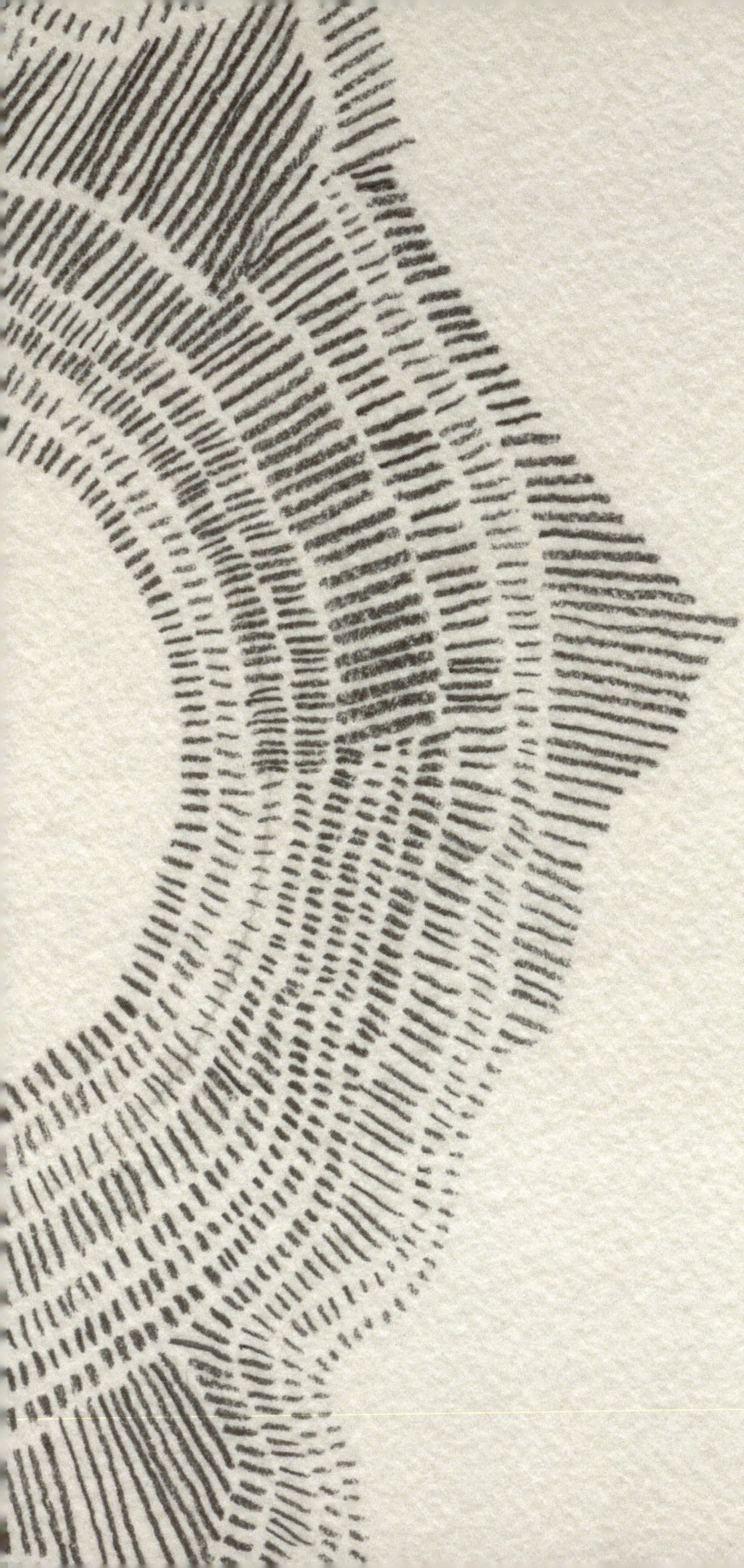

Introduction

Olivia Shao

Of Mythic Worlds: Works from the Distant Past through the Present explores the ways that rituals, myths, traditions, ideologies, and beliefs can intersect across cultures, histories, and time periods. Using an art historical lens that eschews notions of linear progress, this exhibition and publication project highlights how multiple perspectives can coexist. The fifty-three works included in this presentation originate from different places and periods: the earliest examples include a block print from the Qing dynasty (China, 1644-1912) and a nineteenth-century Shaker gift drawing, while other works span the decades from the 1940s to today. The commonalities–both visual and conceptual–that connect the individual histories of these works stem from a universal pursuit to understand that which is outside of our objective, worldly experience.

Investigations in personal belief systems, spirituality, and consciousness are seen in the works of several artists. A number of the works also explore the metaphysical and the sublime, the cosmologies of Tantra and Taoism, and views on mysticism and immateriality. Still other works recall myths passed down from ancient cultures and cross the mystical with cultural narratives.

Several of the featured artists have a writing practice, and others are writers who create art. While language and art both provide a means of communicating ideas, in the instance of art, the visual can often express that which words cannot. As the filmmaker Andrei Tarkovsky wrote: "Artistic images are always a metonym, where one thing is substituted for another...The infinite cannot be made into matter, but it is possible to create an illusion of the infinite: the image... None of this can be understood in any cerebral sense.

The idea of infinity cannot be expressed in words or even described, but it can be apprehended through art, which makes infinity tangible."[1]

Drawing, in particular, and the immediacy with which it connects the brain to the hand, can be a particularly powerful means of expressing one's interior thoughts and perceptions.

Viewers, then, are encouraged to derive their own interpretations and draw their own connections when seeing this exhibition. In the act of looking, a multitude of readings and conclusions can be derived from one's personal experiences, creating unique and meaningful ways of understanding. Art records time and culture, transporting the viewer to the past and into the present, from one dimension to another through the material object. For the duration of the exhibition, and between the covers of this book, the works share a space in time and place where the original meaning and intent of each work is no longer fixed and can evolve to take on new significance, conveying insights and expanding our understanding of history and art.

1 Andrey Tarkovsky, *Sculpting in Time: Reflections on the Cinema* (1986; rept. Austin: University of Texas Press, 2003), 38-39.

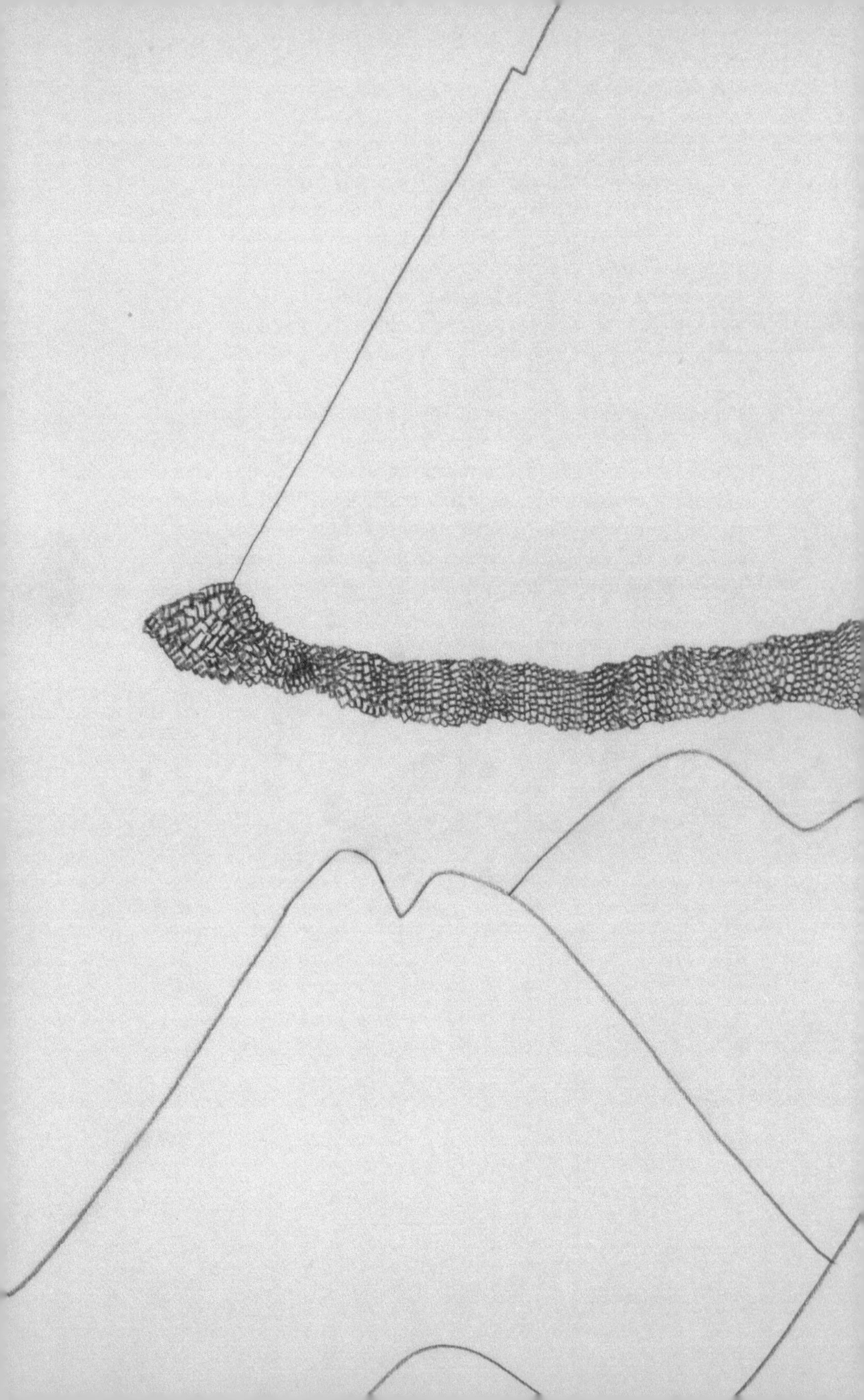

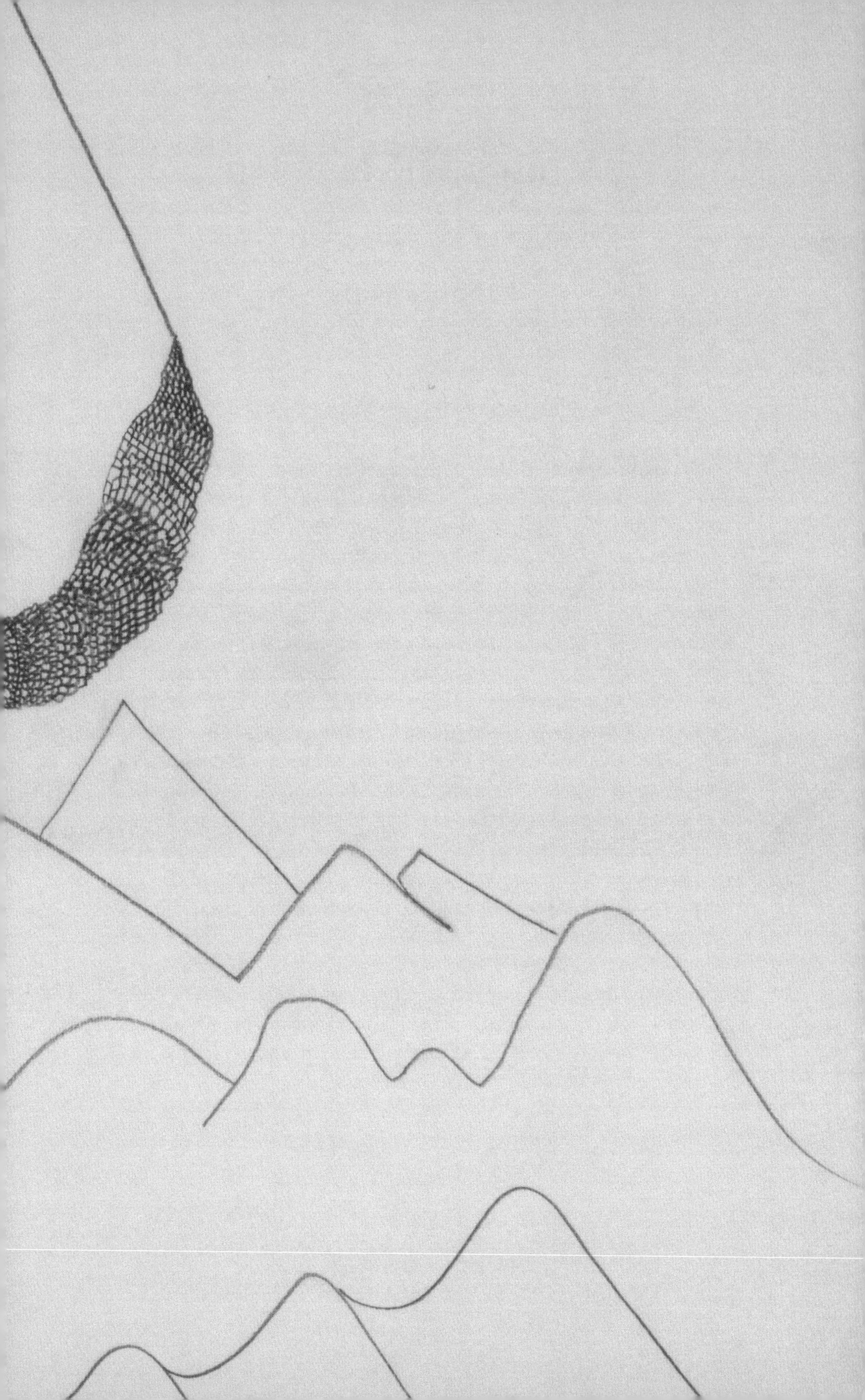

Memory Is Everything

Lauren O'Neill-Butler

Cameron never wanted another gallery show. After Wallace Berman was arrested in 1957 at the Ferus Gallery for showing an "obscene" reproduction of her *Untitled (Peyote Vision)* (1955)–an ink drawing of a fantastical couple copulating–she quit the commercial art scene. Then, as now, rejection is chic. A version of career suicide, Marjorie Cameron Parsons Kimmel's bewitching *no* persisted until her death in 1995: she worked alone, outside of the art world, and incorporated automatist techniques derived from her meditation practices into her works. "Cameron remained steadfast in her creation of art simultaneously with the evolution of her spiritual consciousness, despite the precarious financial circumstances such a peripheral artistic status entailed," as Susan L. Aberth has noted.[1] Cameron, a so-called mystic, has claimed her rightful spot in art history only in the past ten years.

In studies of mysticism, as in art history, the question of what's canonical always nags. Cameron had long been primed for rebirth: her Cimmerian drawings, paintings, and poems were vital contributions to 1950s and '60s counterculture and the occult-friendly Los Angeles milieu. From her undated ink-on-paper illustrations for *Songs of the Witch Woman* (made for a book of poems penned by her husband, rocket engineer and Thelemite Jack Parsons) to her spellbinding late-career abstractions for *Pluto Transiting the Twelfth House* (1978–86) she was certainly one of California's, but also American art's, most vivacious and beguiling heretics.

---

1 Susan L. Aberth, "Spirit Voices, Women's Voices: Art and Mediumship," in Susan L. Aberth, Lars Bang Larsen, and Simon Grant, eds., *Not Without My Ghosts: The Artist as Medium* (London: Hayward Gallery Publishing, 2020), 46.

I begin with Cameron because she's a wonderful entry point to thinking about the mystical tradition and one of the richest themes in this exhibition: the limitations of mortal language. In mysticism, this limit is often connected to the impossibility of fully describing a divine encounter, the impermanence of humanity, and the eternity of the divine.[2] It is also a method of approaching a "withness" or unity with the divine: it bypasses (and sometimes intersects with) philia, eros, and eroticism and takes one out of oneself via a form of *ekstasis*–a "stepping outside" the confines of the self. The mystic's love for the divine, and desire to convey their experience, is an attempt to go beyond mortality into a fused, ecstatic state, which demands a death of the ego. Some of the works in *Of Mythic Worlds* revolve around similar ideas.

One example of this attempt to "speak" the divine is the Shaker gift drawing in the show, *Word of the Saviour* (1843), which graphically records a spiritual vision. The United Society of Believers in Christ's Second Coming–a fascinating British sect brought to America in 1774 by their leader, Ann Lee–became known as Shaking Quakers, or Shakers, for their vivid expression of spirit possession through their ecstatic trances and whirling of "instruments"–which were mostly women. Their visions were transcribed, usually by other women, and presented as gifts to members of the community to provide spiritual encouragement. In these works, there are fragments of recognizable English among mostly inscrutable forms, which recall geometry, musical notation, and traditional American folk-art iconography such as birds, leaves, candles, hearts, fans, and trumpets.

I. Rice Pereira also called herself an instrument. She used the term "rhythms" as early as 1937 to refer to a kind of channeling. While explaining to a *Life* magazine journalist in 1953 what informed both her paintings and her poetry, she observed, "If I don't lose the rhythms, I won't make mistakes." In 1950, she described herself as an "instrument" for creative energies, and in her 1953 unpublished manuscript, *Eastward Journey*, she wrote of herself as a "medium for communication" and, a year later, as a "translator for an inner voice."[3]

---

2 By "divine" I mean to imply the infinite, the non-human, the one, the void, negation, which is here studied as an absent object.

3 Karen Bearor, *Irene Rice Pereira: Her Paintings and Philosophy* (Austin: University of Texas Press, 2011), 169.

On March 17, 1978, Jack Whitten wrote in his studio notebook: "I am beginning to understand that I am in touch with something. I have no other way to express this except 'in touch' . . . Maybe it is what the older people back home call God. Maybe it is what ancient people mean by the spirit, in American Indian terms the 'Great Spirit.' I DO NOT KNOW WHAT IT IS OR WHAT TO CALL IT."[4] Whitten was careful to divorce his art from religion or metaphor, but he was always interested in the spirit and soul of people, and things.

The limitations of mortal language may have prompted Roland Barthes to make over 500 drawings in gouache, crayon, pen, and ink in the 1970s, which remain an understudied part of his life. They've long been cited as visual poetry and as asemic writing (though to say they are entirely without meaning or any semantic content is off). Many of these were made for his lover, Romaric Sulger-Buel. Peter Schwenger has argued that the drawings could be a way of overcoming the problem expressed in Barthes's book *A Lover's Discourse*, wherein he writes, "Love has of course a complicity with my language (which maintains it) but it cannot be lodged in my writing." And so, Schwenger writes, "it is conveyed in these asemic notes that say nothing and everything."[5]

Akin in style to Cameron's quasi-calligraphic *Pluto Transiting the Twelfth House*, Barthes's works on paper are hypnotic. He called them *contre-écritures* (counter-entries), and in April 1976 he published a selection under the heading of *Graphies* in a special issue of the Belgian literary journal *Luna-Park*. His art appeared alongside that of artists now recognized as significant figures in the development of asemic writing, such as Mirtha Dermisache and Brion Gysin. His author's note simply read: "If my graphisms are illegible, it is precisely in order to say No to commentary."

Another celebrated writer who turned to art when faced with the restrictions of language is Janet Malcolm. She made collages from personal effects–letters, postcards, and old photos–and "as time went on, she took them more seriously, and wanted to think of them as art," writes David Salle.[6] Malcolm's fifth solo exhibition at Lori Bookstein Fine Art in New York in 2014 was titled *The Emily*

---

4 Jack Whitten, *Jack Whitten: Notes from the Woodshed*, ed. Katy Siegel (Zurich: Hauser & Wirth Publishers, 2018), 124.

5 Peter Schwenger, *Asemic: The Art of Writing* (Minneapolis: University of Minnesota Press, 2019), 9

6 David Salle, "Janet Malcolm (1934-2021)," *Artforum*, September 2021, https://www.artforum.com/print/202107/david-salle-on-janet-malcolm-86314.

Dickinson Series and offered a collection of her collages assembled with construction paper, glassine, charts, photographs, and shards of poems. The works were inspired by Marta Werner's book *Emily Dickinson's Open Folios: Scenes of Reading, Surfaces of Writing* (1995), which pairs images of Dickinson's late scraps of paper–thought to be drafts of love letters–with Werner's typewritten transcripts on the facing page. In 2012, Malcolm wrote Werner to ask if she might buy a copy of the out-of-print book; Werner responded that she had only one copy left, but that she would be happy to send it along as a gift. Malcolm, grateful for Werner's generosity, accepted and sent her a copy of her own book of photographs of burdock leaves, *Burdock* (2008), as a gift in return. In their correspondence, some of which is included in this volume, Malcolm discloses "the special reason" why she wanted a copy of Werner's text:

> *When I saw the book at Sharon Cameron's house, this desire formed itself in my mind–I began to 'see' the collages. It was the typewritten transcriptions rather than the handwritten originals that stirred my imagination. The series I want to make will also use images and charts from astronomical texts. Before starting the 'cutting' and 'scissoring' (the words leaped out of your text) of your precious only copy, I want to have your permission to do so.*[7]

The conversation continued and became personal and "uncanny" according to both writers. After receiving Werner's consent, Malcolm sent her a few photographs of the first works she made in 2013, in which she had placed lines from Werner's typescripts of Dickinson's words alongside pages from an astronomical book by Nick Lomb titled *The Transit of Venus, 1631 to the Present* (2011). "It seemed almost obligatory that images of stars and planets and moons accompany her gnomic utterances," Malcolm wrote.

One of the scientists whose portrait Malcolm had included in her collages, an astronomer named David Peck Todd, was married to the woman who was in part responsible for the posthumous publication of Dickinson's poems: Mabel Loomis Todd (who had a longtime affair with the poet's brother, Austin Dickinson). In this collage, which is titled *No* (2013), Malcolm placed Todd's picture above Dickinson's

---

7 Janet Malcolm, "The Emily Dickinson Series," *Granta*, no. 126 (January 23, 2014): https://granta.com/the-emily-dickinson-series, and "Janet Malcolm: The Emily Dickinson Series," Lori Bookstein Projects, https://www.booksteinprojects.com/archive/janet-malcom-the-emily-dickinson-series.

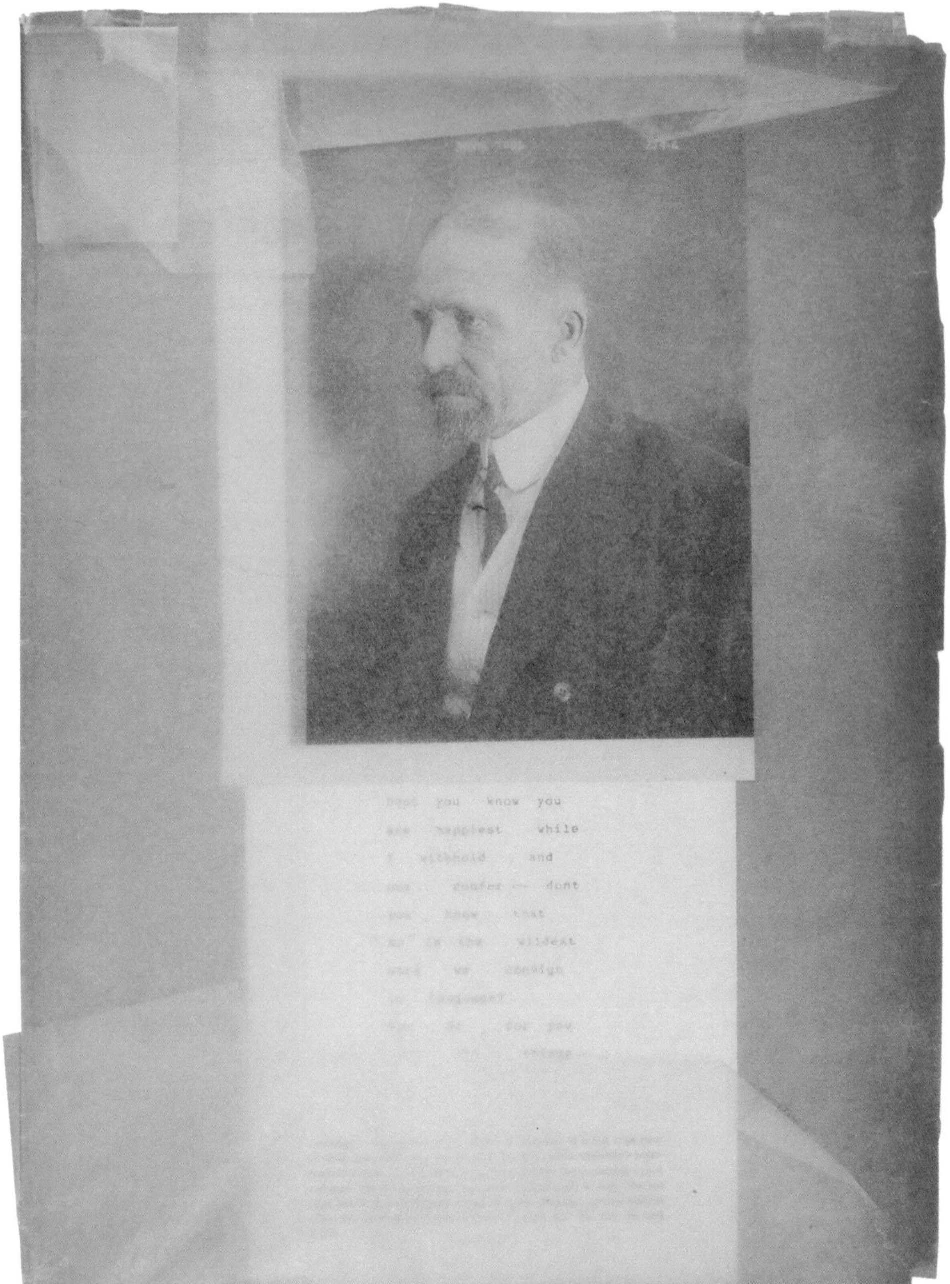

FIG. 1
Janet Malcolm, *No* (from *The Emily Dickinson Series*), 2013

words: "Don't you know you are happiest while I withhold and not confer–don't you know that 'no' is the wildest word we consign to language?"

Werner thought Malcolm must have known this was an image of David Peck Todd, but she didn't. Malcolm wrote to Werner, "There does seem to be something occult going on here, and I don't think I believe in the occult." Werner responded, "I am thrilled to be touched by the uncanny. Like you, I have my doubts about the invisible world, but something strange and lovely may be at work. I did not know of these connections–the Dickinson/Venus transit connections–before I found them in your collages. But I assumed YOU knew." Malcolm wrote back: "What are we to make of my NOT knowing?"

Malcolm's art is one of the only instances of work in this show that is not directly occupied with memory, memoir, or memorial–as in Cici Wu's *The Disappearance of Yu Man-hon (storyboard 02)* (2017), which regards the search for a missing boy and the importance of maintaining the memory of him, and Barbara Chase-Riboud's haunting *The Foley Square Monument New York* (1996) from the *Monument Drawings* series, in which the artist envisioned large-scale public memorials as tributes to figures or sites of importance to her. This piece was made around the time the artist received her first major public commission, for a sculpture to commemorate a burial ground for free and enslaved Africans that had recently been excavated at Foley Square (now the African Burial Ground National Monument).

"The origin of drawing and the origin of painting give rise to multiple representations that substitute memory for perception," writes Jacques Derrida in *Memoirs of the Blind: The Self-Portrait and Other Ruins* (1993), an essay accompanying an exhibition he curated at the Louvre. Here, he argues that drawing originates in the attempt to recapture perception through memory. "First, because they are *re*presentations, next, because they are drawn most often from an exemplary narrative . . . and finally, because the narrative relates the origin of graphic representation to the absence or invisibility of the model."[8]

This is something that many artists know very well. As Whitten once said, "I have always accepted memory as being one of the most

---

8 Jacques Derrida, *Memoirs of the Blind: The Self-Portrait and Other Ruins* (Chicago: University of Chicago Press, 1993), 49.

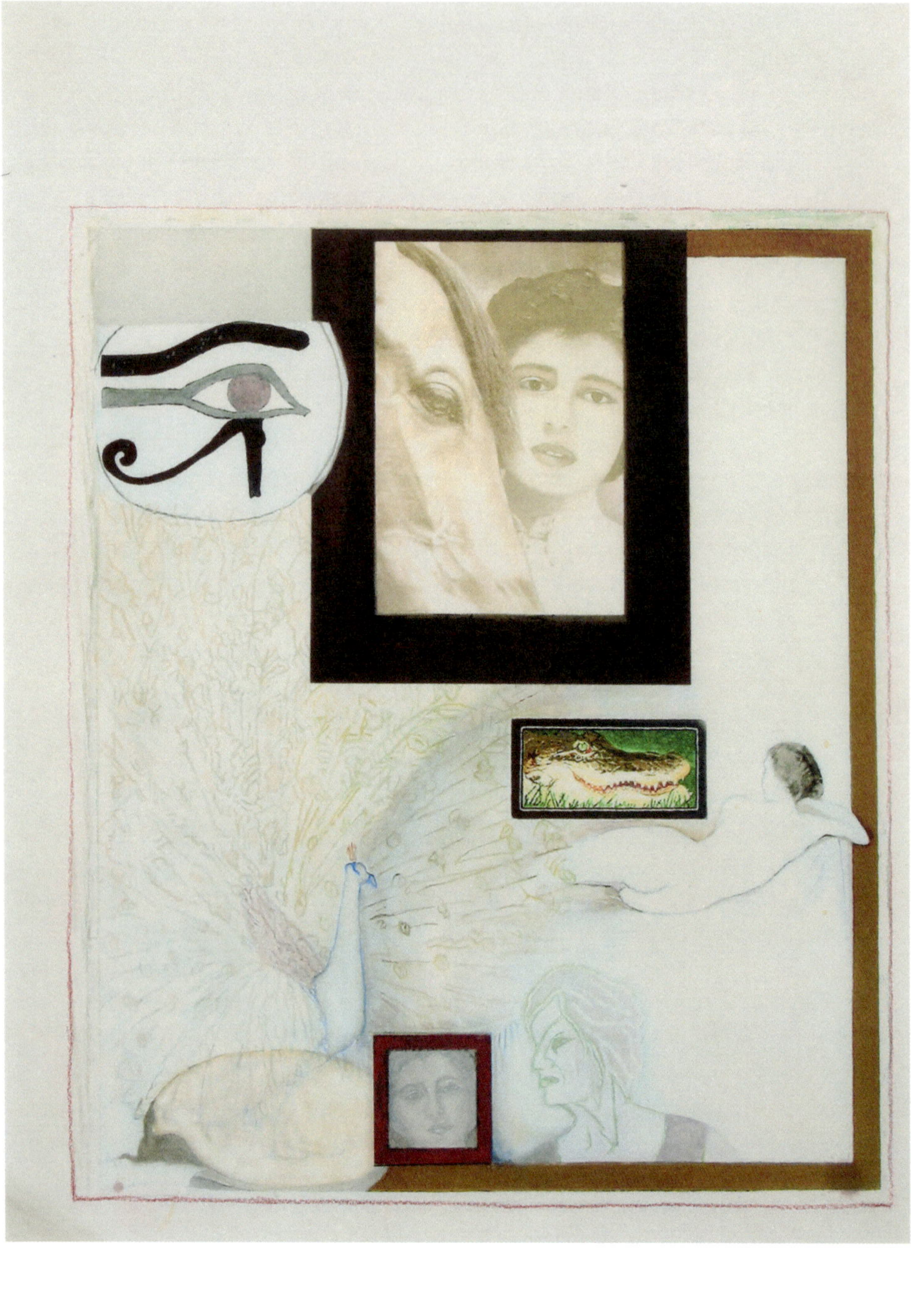

FIG. 2
Jo Baer, *Where I've Been Jo?* (2022)

powerful elements of human consciousness. Through memory we reconstruct our past. We honor the dead through memory."[9] Or, as Chase-Riboud noted, "Memory is everything."[10] In Hannah Arendt's touchstone essay "Thinking and Moral Considerations" she speaks of the idea of *re*presentation in its connection to thinking: "An object of thought is always a re-presentation, that is, something or somebody that is actually absent and present only to the mind which, by virtue of imagination, can make it present in the form of an image."[11]

"I do all my thinking in images," Jordan Belson once said. "I've come to have a complete mistrust of words, and all the fallacious possibilities they contain. It's so easy to get worked up over them. Just a few words can create such a problem."[12] Belson's pictures range from depictions of interior, mental visions to the furthest reaches of the observable universe. "I'm trying to make pictures that focus and teach you about a knowledge that is beyond words," he claimed.[13] Betye Saar's art similarly examines her lived reality, which she understood as just one instantiation out of many possible pasts and futures. Like Belson, Saar was never interested in just one spiritual system and employed many references to the occult and esoteric in her work. In *Taurus*, she uses the astrological sign to create her own personal iconography. Similarly, Jo Baer has long drawn from and manipulated historical imagery to create her own visual lexicon. As she once said: "I wish to use image language that is available. Going to other cultures–the caves, Egyptians, Greeks, Etruscans, whatever–they're interesting images, images that are not usual, not part of every magazine or billboard." She continued: "They're specific but they're speaking different languages, and why not? Our behaviors and interests go all the way back to the caves."[14]

---

9 Jack Whitten, "Jack Whitten in Conversation," interview by Alexander Gray, *Jack Whitten* (New York: Alexander Gray Associates, 2013), 3.

10 Barbara Chase-Riboud, "Memory Is Everything" interview by Hans Ulrich Obrist, *Mousse*, April 10, 2017: https://www.moussemagazine.it/magazine/barbara-chase-riboud-hans-ulrich-obrist-2017/.

11 Hannah Arendt, "Thinking and Moral Considerations," *Social Research* 38, no 3. (Autumn 1971): 424.

12 "Jordan Belson on his art," *The Brooklyn Rail*, December 2014-January 2015, https://brooklynrail.org/2014/12/criticspage/jordan-belson-on-his-art.

13 Ibid.

14 Jo Baer, "A telephone interview," interview by Brian Evans White, 2009, *Jo Baer: Broadsides & Belles Lettres: Selected Writings and Interviews 1965-2010* (Amsterdam: Roma Publications, 2010), 171.

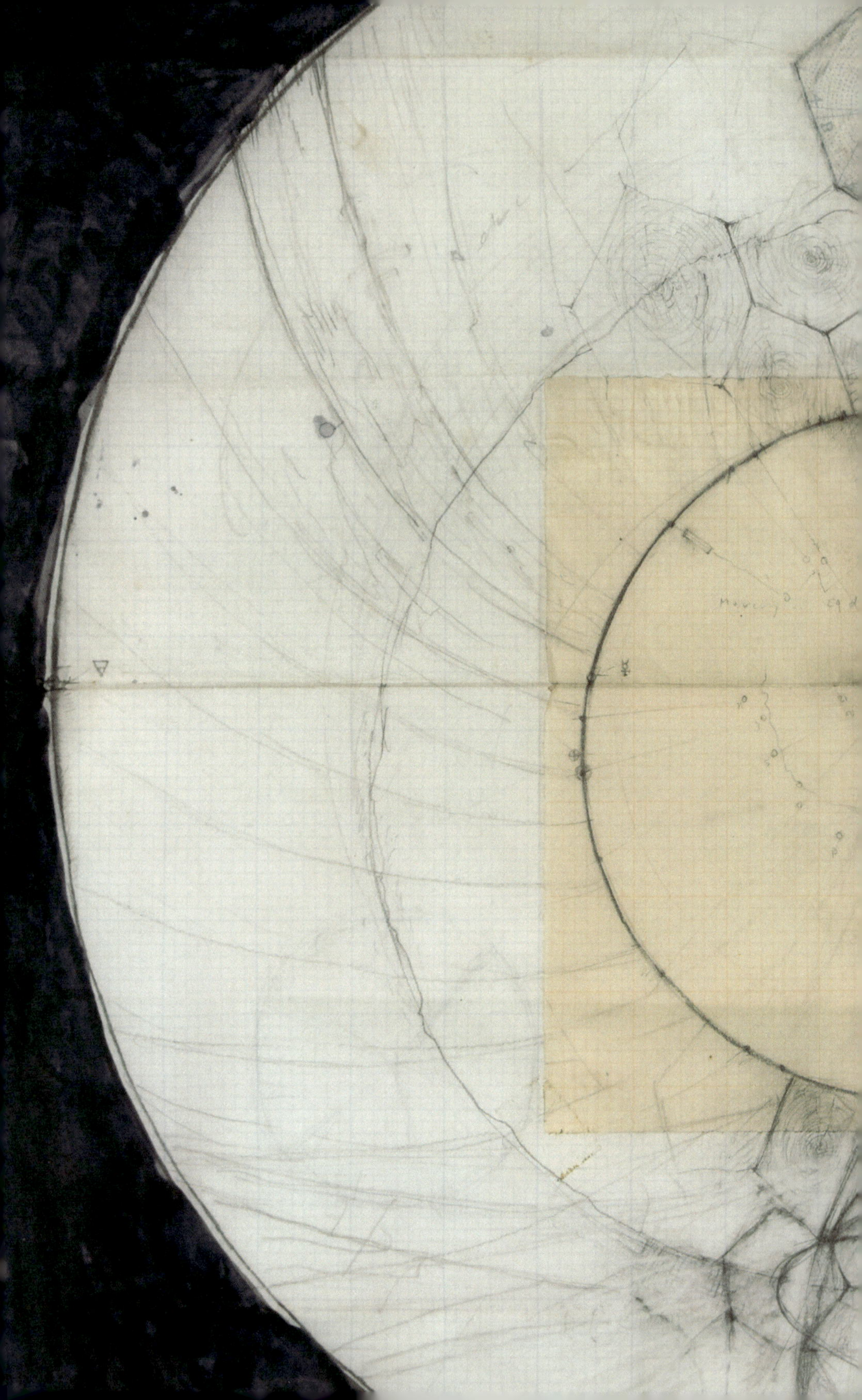

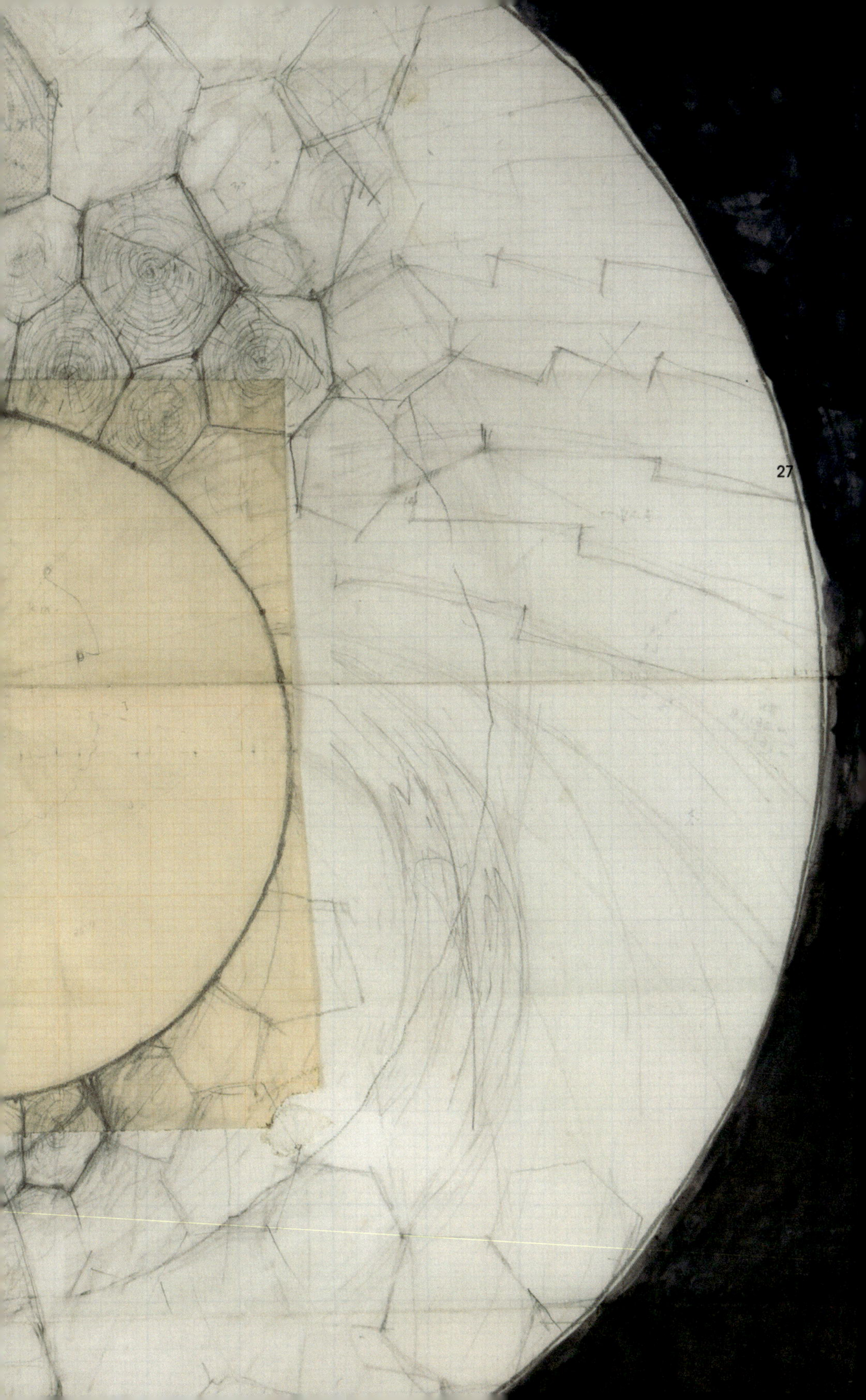

Notes on the Artists

Elise Duryee-Browner
E. C. Feiss
Maya Hayda
Annie Ochmanek
Olivia Shao

Jo Baer

b. 1929, Seattle, Washington

In three of Jo Baer's untitled drawings from 1960, monochromatic, geometric shapes hover on the page in symmetrical relation [PLS. 36–38]. These works exhibit the pared-down formal vocabulary that characterized her early paintings like those in the series called *The Risen* (1960–61/2019). During that period, Baer was interested in physiologies of optical perception, such as the ways in which humans visualize adjacent edges of dark and light colors, and she explored these phenomena in her work. By the mid-1960s, she became a well-known painter amidst the "hard-edge" or "minimalist" artists of the time, and she argued against claims advanced by her sculptor peers Robert Morris, Dan Flavin, and Donald Judd that painting on canvas had lost relevance as an artistic medium.

Beginning in 1975, Baer introduced figurative content to her work, overlaying fragments of imagery traced from disparate sources. Her later paintings incorporate references from the artist's personal archive as well as from her research into Paleolithic, Neolithic, and ancient cultures' religious rites, astrological monuments, and beliefs in the afterlife. *Where I've Been Jo?* (2022) [PAGE 24] combines three animals or perhaps archetypes (a horse, a crocodile, and a peacock) with three portraits of the artist from the past and an anonymous odalisque figure shown from behind. In the upper left corner, Baer rendered the ancient Egyptian hieroglyph that represents the Eye of Horus, which signals healing, protection, and well-being. If her early works explored a sense of balance using abstract forms, this recent work uses the space of painting as a means to put different historical, cultural, and biological iconographies in dialogue. –**AO**

Roland Barthes

b. 1915, Cherbourg-Octeville, France; d. 1980

Throughout the 1970s, literary and social theorist Roland Barthes maintained a regular practice that resulted in several hundred works on paper: sitting at a desk and using pens, pastels, and acrylic paints on small sheets of paper, Barthes drew nets and groupings of marks that sit somewhere between writing and gestural expression.

Given Barthes's advances in the studies of linguistic and cultural sign systems, one can imagine that in these drawings he was exploring the boundaries of what makes a line, or an assembly of gestures, legible as something other than itself [PLS. 4, 5]. No discernible meaning is figured here, though one senses that Barthes is deliberately skirting around its coherence.

Also in the 1970s, Barthes wrote of his interest in similar ambiguities that are featured in the work of artists such as Cy Twombly and André Masson—both artists used scribbles or lines to play at the outskirts of written language and pictorial representation. Barthes also admired Chinese and Japanese calligraphy, which he saw as visibly rendering an energy in excess of a purely linguistic transcription of meaning. Barthes saw this supplementary dimension, which escapes (and thereby reveals) the guidelines of significatory systems, to be a key capacity of art. –**AO**

Jordan Belson

b. 1926, Chicago, Illinois; d. 2011

Jordan Belson, a seminal avant-garde and experimental filmmaker, is best known for his films in which colors and forms, including mandalas and particles of light, shift and expand to create elaborate patterns, often accompanied by synthesized sound. He grew up in San Francisco and received a degree in Studio Art from the University of California, Berkeley. He remained in the North Beach neighborhood of San Francisco for the rest of his life. After attending the "Art in Cinema" screenings at the San Francisco Museum of Modern Art in 1946, he became interested in film. From 1957 to 1959 he collaborated with sound artist Henry Jacobs on a popular series of analog music and light shows at the now all-digital Morrison Planetarium in San Francisco that had substantial influence on both sound design and the psychedelic light shows of the hippie era that followed.

Resisting the characterization of his work as abstract, he explained, "I first have to see the images somewhere, within or without or somewhere... I don't make them up."[1] He experimented with psychedelics, studied Eastern thought and maintained a lifelong yoga practice, all of which contributed to the mind-expanding states that provided inspiration for his artworks. Science, too, was influential in his thinking; color and light played a fundamental role in his films as well as in his paintings and drawings, and he required that everything in his work "make sense from what we know of physics" and retain a connection to the physical world.[2]

The two works titled *Brain Drawing* from 1952 appear to combine both his mysticism and interest in science: cell-like, they also convey vibrations of invisible energy, solar systems, mechanical instruments, and a cosmic symmetry [PLS. 18, 19]. The drawings are mandala-like works that depict a process of interpenetration, perhaps communicating both the mystical quality of the internal processes of the brain's neural connections and the capacity of the brain to perceive the existence of structures in the universe not visible to the eye. The quick calligraphic lines of *Peacock Book Drawing 07* (1952) [PL. 3] seem to relate a similar energy exchange of particles, the more dense and chaotic lines at the top of the painting held in by a cloud-like form from which droplet-like lines rain downward. "Intuition is the basis of my aesthetic judgment," Belson said, "The more you allow intuition to speak to you the closer you are to the truth, and the origins of the universe."[3] –**EDB**

1 Gregory Zinman, "Re-entry: Thoughts on Jordan Belson," *The Brooklyn Rail*, December 2011/January 2012, https://brooklynrail.org/2011/12/film/re-entry-thoughts-on-jordan-belson-19262011.
2 Raymond Foye, "Notes on Jordan Belson," March 18, 2019, https://raymondfoye.info/2019/03/18/notes-on-jordan-belson/.
3 Ibid.

Robert Bittenbender

b. 1987, Washington, DC

In Robert Bittenbender's wall reliefs and hanging sculptures, disparate fragments of trash-matter are pressed and sutured together, some fit within picture frames or rectilinear shapes to outline them, as if to conflate pictorial space and an actual density of things. The jaggedness of the many shards stays palpable, and the parts are visibly separate–tape, wires, zip ties, plastic piping, necklaces, shoes, earrings, innumerable bits and pieces–yet their complex intertwining gives a synthesis to the chaos. Assemblage has a history of partaking in the grit of the urban landscape and the glamour of camp, and Bittenbender's work is no exception.

The detritus and neglect resulting from rampant overproduction is the very matter of his works, while his sculptures are also permeated by a taste for the theatrical.

The material compression and intensity that characterizes his assemblages comes through in Bittenbender's work on paper *Saturina* (2018) [PL. 6]. The pastel picture with pencil striations does not resolve into any one, clear picture or figure-ground relation; instead, we seem to be almost squinting at a vision or hallucination, as if a formal message is emerging from a strong ray of light or radiating energy. The layering and fragmenting of representation in *Saturina* recalls early twentieth-century Cubist portraits, while its mysterious overdrive evokes something more like the presence of deities or an alchemical process of transformation. –**AO**

Lee Bontecou

b. 1931, Providence, Rhode Island

Lee Bontecou grew up in America's Northeast; she often went with her mother from her home in Westchester to see art in New York City, and she spent summers in Nova Scotia exploring the natural world. The Second World War broke out during her youth, and her parents both worked fabricating submarines and gliders for the war effort; the darkness of this war and the many that followed were a fixation for her. After a childhood of drawing and working in clay, she undertook formal studies in art in junior college at the Art Students League and at the Skowhegan School of Painting and Sculpture.

Bontecou's signature reliefs, which press off the wall into a zone between painting and sculpture to create space for the voids at their centers, developed from a drawing experiment she did while studying in Rome on a Fulbright scholarship in her late twenties. While welding she discovered that if she turned off the oxygen on her oxyacetylene torch, she could use the tool to deposit layers of soot on paper, achieving a deep black with tiny particles of carbon. "Getting the black," she explained, "opened everything up. It was like dealing with the outer limits."[1]

The black centers in her sculptures and drawings resemble bodily (orifices), natural (black holes), and mechanical features (jet engines or machined bolt-holes) in turn. That their illusionary depths can appear to lead to an interior or out into eternity results from her efforts to capture both the negativity and optimism of the abyssal potential of the void. Bontecou's lifelong interest in fish and the deep sea as well as planes and outer space took forms both structural (she created vacuum-formed fish and used welded steel sheets in her reliefs) and metaphorical; the ability of fish and planes to traverse substances alien to human life and reach these depths may have made them symbols for her of freedom "in all its necessary ramifications–its awe, beauty, magnitude, horror and baseness."[2]

The graphite-and-soot drawing included here [PL. 51] was created in 1960, the year Bontecou began making reliefs. Unlike the many drawings she made while developing the dimensional structures, this one is signed as an artwork unto itself. Its lidded hole's apparent distance from the paper's surface is accomplished with a series of shaded lines that almost resemble industrial metal scaffolding but for their slightly organic curves and imperfect symmetry. The drawing also recalls an interplay between the natural and mechanical, interior and exterior, speaking to the many ways the membrane of our world might be breached, the lurking, seductive void or voids made visible in these punctures. –**EDB**

1 Lee Bontecou, quoted in Leslie Jones, "Lee Bontecou's Sublime Drawings," *Art on Paper* 8, no. 4 (March/April 2004): 50–53.
2 Ibid.

Cameron

b. 1922, Belle Plain, Iowa; d. 1995

Draftsman, painter, poet, actor, and occult practitioner, the artist Cameron was a visionary cross-disciplinary creator as well as an influential member of the postwar Los Angeles counterculture and avant-garde.

Cameron's life has been the subject of much fascination. Born in Iowa in 1922 as Marjorie Elizabeth Cameron, she enlisted in the Navy as a cartographer and wardrobe mistress after high school. Following her discharge from the Navy, she moved to Pasadena in 1945. It was in Pasadena that Cameron began to enter occult circles, encountering and later marrying Jack Parsons, a cofounder of the Jet Propulsion Laboratory, avid pupil of Aleister Crowley, and practitioner of Thelema, the occult and religious movement founded by Crowley. Parsons introduced Cameron to various esoteric practices, including kabbalah, tarot, astrology, and the I Ching, and following his mysterious death in 1952, she delved fully into her own explorations of magick and the occult. Cameron's work as an actor, writer, and artist was greatly influential in the Los Angeles underground; she appeared in several seminal experimental films, including Kenneth Anger's 1954 film *Inauguration of the Pleasure Dome,* and collaborated with Aya (Tarlow), Wallace Berman, George Herms, David Meltzer, and other members of the LA beatnik scene.

Activated as visual conduits of Cameron's own powerful practice as an occultist, her paintings and drawings are deeply influenced by themes of metamorphosis and myth, using line and form to reach into the depths of the psyche to explore "ideas of mystical transcendence."[1] The *Lion Path* series and *Pluto Transiting the Twelfth House* are works from later in Cameron's life and provide glimpses into a kind of mapping of Cameron's own psyche. In *Pluto Transiting the Twelfth House,* she specifically cites a position in the zodiac when one begins to reflect on death and past lives [PL. 29]. The *Lion Path* series references Egyptian astrology and reincarnation [PLS. 46–48]. Created under the spell of hypnosis and employing automatist techniques, both works are contingent with a different kind of consciousness linked to a transcendent transformation of the self. –MH

1 Michael Duncan, "Cameron," the website of the Cameron-Parsons Foundation Inc., http://www.cameron-parsons.org/cameron.html.

Barbara Chase-Riboud

b. 1939, Philadelphia, Pennsylvania

The representation of world-historical narrative—whether and how to present myth, fact, or feeling—can be seen throughout Chase-Riboud's sprawling oeuvre, which encompasses both the literary and visual arts. Her six novels, published between 1979 and 2022, all begin with an event or person critical to the history of the Black diaspora. She was the first to write significantly about the 1839 revolt on the Amistad slavers' ship (*Echo of Lions*, 1989) and her resurrection of the story of enslaved woman Sally Hemings (*Sally Hemings: A Novel*, 1979) utilized archival material to describe—against mainstream academic consensus—Hemings's thirty-eight-year relationship with Thomas Jefferson. Historians disputed Chase-

Riboud's Hemings story upon publication, but in the 1990s DNA evidence proved the artist's intuition correct. It is now commonly accepted that Hemings was the mother of Jefferson's six children. Chase-Riboud's poetic confirmation of what was later qualified by science, a literary blurring of fiction and fact enabled by the artist's deep reading of Hemings's trace in the archive, fittingly introduces the investments of her artwork. Indeed, she consistently discusses her writing and artwork as inseparable.

In the *Monument Drawings* series (1996–97) Chase-Riboud uses multiple methods for making lines–etching, drypoint, ink, and pencil–to depict unreal, cavernous monoliths dedicated to people, sites, and events. Some of the *Monument Drawings* are dedicated to, for example, the Russian poet Anna Akhmatova, who lived and wrote during Stalin's reign (*Akhmatova's Monument*, 1996); the artist Man Ray; the space and time of the middle passage, the cross-Atlantic journey that delivered captured people from Western Africa to the Americas (*Middle Passage Monument*, 1997). These impossible structures, their joints and foundations hazily rendered, announce themselves immediately as anti-blueprints, never to be built. The intricate print-drawing *The Foley Square Monument New York* is distinct in that it corresponds–like a dreamscape version–to the artist's first public commission for which she installed a bronze sculpture (*Africa Rising*, 1998) in the foyer of Foley Square's federal building [PL. 50].[1] Both works–on paper and in bronze–refer to the eighteenth-century African burial ground under the Square: *Africa Rising* is a strident figure, laden with references to African craft (textiles and masks) yet rendered in a classically Western shape and finish. By contrast, the *Foley Square Monument* drawing is ethereal and indistinct. A tomb entrance or perhaps a celestial portal, the drawing forgoes the West African symbols and the Western heroic frame Chase-Riboud employed in her bronze depiction of the enslaved. Instead, the drawing asks how such an immense collective trauma as embedded in the burial ground might be remembered, inviting viewers to ruminate on the afterlife as well as the history of the afterlife as a concept, an idea at least as old as the Egyptian or Etruscan tombs the work alludes to. –**ECF**

1 The artist bemoaned aspects of the federal commission: "In order to see the sculpture you have to get through security. There is somebody standing there with guns while you walk around it" ("Memory is Everything: Barbara Chase-Riboud in Conversation with Hans Ulrich-Obrist," *Mousse*, April 10, 2017, https://www.moussemagazine.it/magazine/barbara-chase-riboud-hans-ulrich-obrist-2017/). Her dissatisfaction with the conditions of memorialization require that the two works–*Africa Rising* and *The Foley Square Monument New York*–be understood together.

Mel Chin

b. 1951, Houston, Texas

Utilizing structures of Conceptual Art, Mel Chin's multi-layered work examines a range of complex political, social, historical, and spiritual ideas. In his multi-disciplinary practice, Chin works across drawing, painting, sculpture/objects, installation, multimedia, and technology. According to Chin, his work mostly originates through concepts, although they can spring "from dreams, which then connects with the nightmares of the 'mean events' and surreal events in the works, and is brought into reality, to create the final artwork."[1]

The works included in this exhibition explore Chinese Taoist philosophy, alchemy, cultural histories of New York, and the environment. *Garden where the Wild Grass Obscures the True Pearl* (1987) is a proposal drawing for a site-specific park located on Canal and Forsyth Streets in New York City's Chinatown [PL. 1]. Chin applied Taoist feng shui ideals and considered the ethnic Chinese inhabitants when determining the design and layout of the park. The drawing depicts the park in the shape of an oyster, pointing to New York City's history–specifically that New York harbor was once surrounded by hundreds of miles of oyster reefs. Within the oyster drawing is a metaphorical pearl, marking the location where a homeless man had made a shelter. Even before the shelter was dismantled by authorities, a feng-shui master suggested altering the flow of qi by burying the debris on site, transmuting trash into treasure, and commemorating the one-time shelter as a hidden "pearl." A sketch of a Taoist talisman (*fu*) in the drawing utilizes the eight trigrams of the Ba Gua and the duality of yin and yang energy, which is the foundation for Taoist metaphysical theory and cosmological principles.

Study for Mercury: The Principle of Polarity–The Orbital Rebus (1987) is a study for a large sculpture, part of the installation *Operation of the Sun through the Cult of the Hand*, an investigation into the origin of word, form, and material through myth, alchemy, astronomy, and science from both Chinese and Greek texts [PL. 27]. The drawing illustrates the shape of inner orbital space, of Mercury's and Earth's rotational paths around the sun. Chin took inspiration from Descartes's illustration of vortices and the solar system,

Kekulé's dream of the benzene ring, and ancient objects such as the Cornish Mên-an-Tol and Chinese Shang Dynasty jade *bi* discs. In Chinese Taoist traditions, mercury is believed to be the elixir of life, possessing longevity and immortality. Within this esoteric practice, mercury is ingested to strengthen the body to attain the cosmic state; due to the material's ability to change from a liquid to solid state, mercury is also thought to transcend life and death, heaven and earth.

Tantra Dream Diagram (1991) [PL. 2] is part of the work *Degrees of Paradise*, which is a study for *The State of Heaven*, a larger installation that explores environmental issues, including the destruction of the ozone layer. The image emerged from a dream of an animated topological equation; painted on paper and mounted on an antique roofing slate, the artwork portrays the earth's atmosphere as the "unfolding petals of a fragile flower."[2]

The works in this exhibition reinterpret and subvert historical ideas and explore Eastern and Western philosophy. Chin brings issues of modern life to the forefront, and in doing so he investigates the ways in which art is activism that can bring about awareness and social engagement. –OS

1 Marcia Brennan, *Do Not Ask Me: Mel Chin* (Houston: Ineri Publishing, Station Museum of Contemporary Art, 2011), 36.

2 Mel Chin, Exhibition flyer for *Degrees of Paradise: The State of Heaven*, Storefront for Art and Architecture, September 13-October 26, 1991, 2.

Walter De Maria

b. 1935, California; d. 2013

Walter De Maria's practice is difficult to categorize, as it touches upon tenets of various art historical movements from Fluxus and Conceptual Art to Land Art and Minimalism. His work investigates complex realities in time and space as well as nature and its underlying forces of energy, spirituality, and invisibility. These themes can be traced in De Maria's drawings from the 1960s, his early sculptures and instructional drawings, and his large-scale Land Art pieces.

De Maria's 1960s drawings depict his subjects–mountains, cats, castles, etc.–with the restraint of only a few lines or the faintest mark on a page. The subtlety of these drawings conveys a profound depth and discipline, a controlled energy transferred from the artist's hand to a line on paper. In an interview with Paul Cummings, De Maria discussed these works: "It wasn't necessary to have a lot of brushstrokes to have a lot of expressionist action. Even with a ruler and one or two lines or just a very, very few lines like the outline of the mountain, it was possible to make a very fine drawing which was almost as much of an idea as it was a drawing."[1]

Floating Mountain (1961–64) is a mysterious and powerful drawing [PL. 12]. The austerity of the line conveys a mountain range with a single suspended mountain above, alluding to the sublime and otherworldly dimensions. Throughout different histories and cultures, mountain imagery has represented divine inspiration and cosmologies; it can also suggest spiritual development and a gateway to other worlds, both physically and metaphorically.

The connective thread throughout De Maria's work is a universal, invisible energy and a spiritual principle. An example of the manifestation of this guiding force, *Floating Mountain* implies something beyond its image—leaving viewers to decipher meaning by reflecting on their own existence. –OS

1 Paul Cummings, Oral history interview with Walter De Maria, October 4, 1972, Archives of American Art, Smithsonian Institution.

Ilka Gedő

b. 1921, Budapest, Hungary; d. 1985

Ilka Gedő, the only child of intellectual and artistically-inclined Jewish parents, drew and painted with great seriousness for nearly her entire life, interrupted substantially by an extended hiatus beginning in her late twenties—often the most productive period in an artist's life. Gedő's father and mother both held jobs and also translated German literary works into Hungarian, so Gedő grew up amidst Hungarian poets and thinkers. She diligently filled sketchbooks with drawings of landscapes, peasants at work, portraits and self-portraits, and city scenes; the earliest extant drawings date from when she was eleven. In the early 1940s Gedő participated in a group exhibition and received a prize for her artistic achievements.

Following the Nazi occupation of Hungary in 1944 her family was forcibly relocated to the Jewish Ghetto in Budapest, where she drew its inhabitants. Some members of their circle died in the

Holocaust, but her immediate family survived and were able to return to their home in 1945, the same year that she met her future husband.

Explorations from Gedő's brief postwar productive period demonstrate her persistent interest in figuration despite the exhortations of her intellectual circle, whose members aimed to achieve a modern approach to art that was associated primarily with abstraction. Lack of artistic recognition–a result of this refusal to create work that appealed to the artistic values of her time, including those of the communist regime–and frustrations with what Gedő called the "unbridgeable gap between artistic work and femininity"[1] combined to produce a lifelong struggle with her own identity as an artist.

Untitled (table #2) is one of a series of fourteen drawings from 1949 (the year Gedő stopped making art) of the same delicate table, its top covered in a patterned cloth and holding on opposite corners a small vase with flowers and a simple teacup. *Untitled (table #2)* is among the most abstract of these drawings [PL. 7]. The pencil lines exude an intense energy: the legs of the table and cloth have been doubled, capturing the movement of a shaking table, whereas the other objects–like remnants or floating essences–have vibrated frenetically off the table's surface. The teacup, in its ascent, becomes a circle. Most strange, perhaps, is the dark, smudged, second circle contained within the lower teacup, hard with the gravity that a table resists when it lifts objects off the ground. –**EDB**

1 Istvan Hajtu and David Biro, *The Art of Ilka Gedő* (Budapest: Gondolat Kiado, 2003).

Morris Graves

b. 1910, Fox Valley, Oregon; d. 2001

The work of Morris Graves draws from the artist's lifelong fascination with the natural world, Eastern philosophy, and religious practices including Zen Buddhism, Taoism, and Hinduism in addition to a personal belief in the spirituality implicit in everyday life and the power of consciousness as a path for self-realization. As Graves expressed, "I paint to evolve a changing language of symbols with which to rear upon the qualities of our mysterious capacities which direct us toward ultimate reality...to verify the inner eye."[1]

Graves was born outside of Seattle and lived most of his life in the Pacific Northwest. Primarily self-taught, his interest in the natural world and Eastern philosophy originated in his youth. Having dropped out of high school after his second year, he found a job as a steamship hand on an eastern-bound ship, exploring Japan, China, and Manila before returning to Seattle in his twenties to pursue a life as an artist. In 1933, his work won first prize at the Northwest Annual Exhibition, an achievement that led to Graves's participation in shows at the Seattle Art Museum and the Museum of Modern Art, New York. In 1936, Graves began painting for the WPA's Federal Art Project, where he met painter Mark Tobey. The two shared similar interest in the metaphysical and in East Asian religious and philosophical practices. Graves and Tobey would go on to be associated with the Northwest School, a group of artists known for their modernist tendencies and use of muted colors and elements of mysticism.[2]

Chalice (1942) reflects Graves's connection to spirituality and enlightenment [PL. 52]. In it, the silhouette of a chalice form is highlighted by a white orb and outline, and by the composition's textural juxtapositions. For Graves, the chalice was a recurring motif, symbolizing a container for the soul and a vehicle for the spirit. The chalice is an emblem of Graves's worldview, which was rooted in the belief that an essential bond exists between individuals and their immediate physical surroundings, a parallel to the interrelation of human souls and forces in divine realms. Graves's chalice is "the cup that holds neither one opposite nor the other but both simultaneously...articulated out of the stuff which apparently surrounds it, i.e., the symbolizing of unity–or of the phenomenal being the illusory projection of consciousness..."[3] –**MH**

1 Morris Graves, quoted in Dorothy Miller, ed., *Americans, 1942: 18 Artists from 9 States*, exh. cat. (New York: The Museum of Modern Art, 1942), 51.

2 The Northwest School was not an institution, rather it is a categorization derived from a 1953 article in *Life* magazine entitled "Mystic Painters of the Northwest." The article featured works and biographies of Morris and Tobey as well as Guy Anderson and Kenneth Callahan, artists now known as the "Big Four" of the Northwest School. "Modernism in the Pacific Northwest: The Mythic and The Mystical," the website of the Seattle Art Museum, 2014, https://www.seattleartmuseum.org/exhibitions/modernism.

3 Graves's studies of Taoism, Zen Buddhism, and Hinduism also inflect his use of the chalice. In 1952, the artist wrote of the vessel as "karmic...the contents of which either pain or Spirit, traditionally is unalterable and/or cannot be ultimately rejected." Graves, under the pseudonym Pauline Governor, in a letter to Virginia Harriman written in Edmonds, WA, December 1, 1952, reproduced in Vicki Halper and Lawrence Fong, eds., *Morris Graves: Selected Letters* (Seattle: University of Washington Press, 2013), 280.

Hu Zhengyan

b. 1584, Xiuning, China; d. 1674

Hu Zhengyan was a traditional Chinese painter, calligrapher, seal-carver, and publisher during the Ming and Qing dynasties in China. He founded the Ten Bamboo Studio in Nanjing, where he explored early color woodblock printing. His most well-known work, *The Ten Bamboo Studio Manual of Calligraphy and Painting*, was first printed in 1633. The work was created in volumes, each devoted to a form of natural imagery–rocks, flowers, birds, fruit, etc.–with contributions by thirty artists (including Hu) working at the time. The print depicting the character and shape of a rock [PL. 054] is reflective of the Taoist belief that the rock is a symbol of wisdom, change, and the power of nature. Contemplating the image of a rock and its form is a reflecting on the spirit and essence of our existence.

In Chinese culture, rocks have inspired for centuries with their poetic nature, spiritual qualities, and concentration of energy. Existing long before us and also long after us, rocks are connected to our conception of the universe and are believed to store and capture qi–the fundamental life-force and universal flow of energy that is the foundation of Taoist thought.

Since the Song dynasty (960-1279) *gongshi*, which can be translated to "spirit rocks," have been admired and collected by the Chinese literati. They are thought to be imbued with a vitality, force, and history, recalling a mountain in miniature. Rocks are an embodiment of the passing of time and the state of impermanence, representing the balance between humans and nature, and heaven and earth. According to the literati, the metaphysical qualities of a rock convey a wisdom that encourages us to both look inward and seek inspiration from the natural world. –OS

Steffani Jemison

b. 1981, Berkeley, California

Steffani Jemison's work reminds viewers of the necessity, and the difficulties, of keeping alive concepts of utopia in the present day. For *Black Utopia (Sol)* (2017), she illustrates this idea with a partially obscured sun [PL. 44]. This evocative image is in fact appropriated from the upper right corner of a book cover—that of William Pease and Jane Pease's 1963 *Black Utopia: Negro Communal Experiments in America*. The Peases' book details several histories, including successes and failures, of organized communities that provided mutual aid for free African Americans and fugitive enslaved people during the antebellum period, such as the Port Royal Experiment in South Carolina and the Dawn Settlement in Ontario.

Once cropped and expanded in Jemison's print, the gestural marks that pass over the "sun" are transformed into unidentifiable, glyph-like fragments. This recalls other instances in which the artist has used unconventional sign systems in her work, such as the ulterior code handwritten by James Hampton or the nineteenth-century musical language called Solresol; the former was a mode of clandestine personal expression, while the latter aimed to be a means of communication fully transparent to all listeners regardless of dialect. For Jemison, the medium of drawing is akin to such coded linguistic systems as well as to projects of world-building. As she wrote, "I am looking for—no, I am looking at—a path to drawing that is a labor and performance of freedom. I am thinking about the relationship between freedom and withdrawal."[1] —**AO**

1 Steffani Jemison, with Introduction by Huey Copeland, "Drafts: Steffani Jemison on the Stroke, the Glyph, and the Mark," *Artforum*, April 2019, 153.

Arnold J. Kemp

b. 1968, Boston, Massachusetts

Arnold J. Kemp is an artist, writer, and educator whose practice spans poetry, painting, sculpture, photography, and performance. Utilizing a variety of media and delving into the historical and metaphorical meanings of materials, from aluminum foil to polished black shoe leather, Kemp's work examines ideas about history and identity. Through encounters with and manipulations of objects such as masks and photographs, Kemp explores psychic symbolizations and their resonance within culture.

Index (2021), a haunting and enigmatic work on paper, is a print of an aluminum sheet, which Kemp had previously molded into a three-dimensional mask, then flattened on a printing press, and inked to create a print [PL. 43].[1] The resulting image is deeply textured, an imprint in black ink on gray wove paper that was handmade at the turn of the nineteenth century. With two eyes and an open mouth, *Index* evokes a human visage frozen in mid-articulation, an abstracted face with spectral traces of a past being.

The handmade paper comes with its own history, adding another layer of significance to the work. Similarly, aluminum, a material that is both industrial and domestic, has a memory of its own kind deriving from its endless plasticity. A flat sheet of foil becomes crinkled, profoundly impressed by the quick movement of a hand, leaving vestiges of prior action. As critic Stephanie Snyder has suggested, Kemp's engagement with foil further deploys its metaphoric potential, using "foil as a foil, to deflect menace, to fool and outsmart violence and predatory behavior, and to protect what is most critical, vulnerable, and precious: art, queer love, blackness, rage, justice."[2]

The mask is an object that incites a dialectic of looking and being looked at.[3] Each act is mediated by the foil barrier, which protects, shields, obscures. A center crease from previous folding bisects *Index*, further instilling the work with the tension of seeing and being seen. The work's title, *Index*, suggests that the piece results from a direct impression or indexical likeness of an individual's face, but Kemp's index goes through a series of modifications, literalizing the refiguration of a visage. The malleability of the foil elicits a feeling of precarity, as *Index* is ultimately a permutated imprint of experiences, inscribed histories ,and psyches. –**MH**

1 "Arnold J. Kemp, "Talking To The Sun" at M. LeBlanc, Chicago," *Mousse*, April 20, 2022, https://www.moussemagazine.it/magazine/arnold-j-kemp-talking-to-the-sun-at-m-leblanc-chicago/.

2 Stephanie Snyder, "Arnold Kemp: FOILING," 2019, the website of Arnold Joseph Kemp, http://a-j-kemp.com/index.php?/texts/foiling-by-stephanie-snyder/.

3 Masks have occupied a large part of Kemp's practice since the 1990s. Angelica Villa, "With a Fred Flintstone Rubber Disguise, Artist Arnold Kemp Explores What Masks Really Reveal," *ARTNews*, April 6, 2022, https://www.artnews.com/art-news/artists/arnold-j-kemp-neubauer-collegium-exhibition-1234622883/.

Mohammed O. Khalil

b. 1936, Burri, Khartoum, Sudan

Mohammed Omer Khalil began painting during his childhood and later graduated with a painting degree from Khartoum's School of Fine and Applied Arts (1959). He then began teaching at the school, eventually becoming head of painting. In the early 1960s, like many North African and Middle Eastern artists of this generation, he moved to Italy for graduate study. At the Academy of Fine Arts in Florence, he was trained in a range of new methods, including mosaic, fresco painting, and printmaking. He attributes this period to the diversification of his two-dimensional practice, and turn, especially, to printmaking. After returning to Khartoum briefly, Khalil moved to New York in 1967, where he still lives and works. While his practice spans multiple media in two dimensions, including collage and painting, he is most well-known for his richly textured prints. He is also a master printmaker who has created prints for artists such as Louise Nevelson and Romare Bearden. Combining Western modernist influences (like Miro and Rauschenberg) with what he termed an "African sensibility," Khalil's oeuvre presents a modern African subjectivity, shaped by his movements between Sudan and the West, and the intricate, suprapersonal, and ongoing experience of diaspora.[1]

Upon arriving in New York City, Khalil studied and worked at Bob Blackburn's Printmaking Workshop, a seminal institution for printmaking and graphic arts in the United States that was founded in 1948. Like many associated with the Workshop, Khalil began to combine printmaking methods in single compositions, using silkscreen over etching or collaged elements with lithography. Through the late 1970s, all of his work was in black and white, utilizing a range of print techniques to ruminate on the two tones and their contrast. He also incorporated found objects and debris found on the street in dense, complex assemblages that reflect upon the lifecycle of the city. In an interview with the artist Camille Billops in the mid-1980s, Khalil spoke of his black-and-white compositions as concerned with African identity but without "obvious African or Moslem (sic) iconography. Some have said that it is not really African."[2] In works like *Bomb Cantata* (1968) [PL. 40] and *The Second Queen* (1974) [PL. 42] marbled black ink swirls in different densities, tones, and textures, reading like granite or lava. For Khalil, the color black expands to hold many concurrent meanings, both social and formal. As he put it: "In blackness, I see degrees and shades of rich, complicated color, more intense than in other colors, roaring and loud."[3] –ECF

1 Camille Billops, "An Interview with Mohammad Khalil," *Black American Literature Forum* 22, no. 1 (1988): 65.

2 Ibid.

3 Charbel Dagner, *Mohammed Omar Khalil: 50 years of Printmaking* (Bahrain: ALBareh Art Gallery, 2013), 89, http://www.contemporarypractices.net/essays/volumeXIV/Mohammed%20Omar%20Khalil.pdf.

Duane Linklater

b. 1976, Moose Cree First Nation, Canada

Born in 1976 in Moose Cree First Nation, Linklater is Omaskêko Ininiwak. Linklater's work interrogates the physical and ideological structures of museums and institutions, and how these structures relate to the current and historical conditions of Indigenous peoples, their practices, and their approaches to materials and cultural objects. Through a range of mediums, including sculpture, video, prints, photography, and installation, Linklater exposes stereotypical and contradictory depictions of Indigenous culture, their social and economic ramifications, and the ways in which they have contributed to the destabilization and disenfranchisement of Indigenous people. Indeed, "Linklater has described his methodology as an 'excavation' of the aggregated 'pile' of misrepresentations that circumscribe Indigenous subjectivities."[1]

In the trio of *Migraine* drawings (2022) that Linklater created especially for this exhibition, he directly subverts the assumption of an implicit spirituality in his work based his identity as an Indigenous artist [PLS. 15, 16, 17]. The aura that Linklater explores in this series is not a mystical ambiance steeped in myth or otherworldliness but a depiction of the visions and shapes he sees while afflicted by migraines. Created in a kind of altered state, the drawings depict visions that are inaccessible in daily consciousness and reflect an abiding interconnection between the self, the psyche, and the surrounding atmosphere.

In *break up swept up all of the willows 1* (2022), Linklater combines crushed cochineal and sumac with acrylic paint [PL. 13]. Both cochineal and sumac have long been used in various cultures to create dyes and paints, and in these works, Linklater explores the same materials in an experiment of mark-making and movement, expanding his artistic vocabulary in connection to the natural world. —**MH**

1 Amanda Donnan, ed., *Duane Linklater: mymothersside*, exh. cat. (Seattle: Frye Art Museum, 2021), 30.

Janet Malcolm

b. 1934 Prague, Czechoslovakia; d. 2021

Widely-known as a writer and journalist, Malcolm was also a photographer and artist. She created collage works that juxtapose imagery, photography, texts, and ephemera. *Ermine* (2013) [PL. 25] and *Cleopatra* (2013) [PL. 26] are part of Malcolm's *Emily Dickinson Series*, in which she incorporates Dickinson's original writings and typed transcriptions from Marta Werner's *Emily Dickinson's Open Folios: Scenes of Reading, Surfaces of Writing.* Malcolm arranges the texts in beautifully sparse compositions with photographs from astronomy books, making a connection to the metaphysical.

Below is a correspondence between Malcolm and Marta Werner, and a text written by Malcolm describing these collages in her own words. –OS

The Emily Dickinson Series: A Correspondence

When I first opened Marta Werner's *Emily Dickinson's Open Folios* I felt a shiver of interest and desire such as one feels in an expensive shop at the sight of an object of particular beauty and rarity. I was drawn to the book's right-hand pages on which typewritten words appeared - words that were wild and strange, and typing that evoked the world of the early-twentieth-century avant-garde. These were Marta Werner's transcriptions of scraps of handwritten prose by Emily Dickinson, discovered after her death. The scraps themselves were reproduced in facsimile opposite the typed transcripts.

The book belonged to my friend Sharon Cameron, a professor and critic and the author of two books on Emily Dickinson that are considered classics in the field. I was at her apartment. She had shown me the book - I forget for what reason - and I asked if I could cut out some of the right-hand pages to put into collages. She looked at me in horror and said, 'Certainly not.'

I tried to buy the book on Amazon and found it was out of print, and couldn't find it anywhere else. Sharon Cameron suggested I write to Marta Werner:

18 September 2012

Dear Marta Werner, I have been trying to purchase a copy of your wonderful book Emily Dickinson's Open Folios, *and have had no success. My friend Sharon Cameron suggested I write to you on the off chance that you had an extra copy I could buy from you, or that you could direct me to a source.*

With thanks and best wishes, Janet Malcolm

Dear Janet Malcolm, How extremely kind of you to write! It's rather strange, I suppose, but I have only one copy of the book. I believe my mother has one, too, though, so since there's one floating about the family somewhere, I'd be happy to send you my copy. I certainly don't want anything for it.

If you'd accept my copy, I'd be delighted to send it. It seems to belong to another part of my life - I hope I learned from it!

All my best, Marta

19 September 2012

Dear Marta, I cannot tell you how moved I am by your offer to give me your only copy of the book. Your generosity is staggering. Of course, I accept with enormous pleasure and gratitude. May I, in inadequate return, send you a copy of my book Burdock, *a collection of photographs of burdock leaves that grew in the New England countryside? If so, would you send me your mail address? My address is [. . .].*

With huge thanks and all best wishes, Janet

Dear Janet, Thank you so much for accepting the book. It is a small thing, after all, and I fear you will definitely lose in this trade. Please don't regret it too deeply!

Of course, I would be delighted to have Burdock *- and it could not come at a better time. I am just starting work on the field notebooks of a rather obscure early twentieth-century naturalist - Cordelia Stanwood - and your photographs - and especially your essay - will press me forward through uncertain beginnings. My address is [. . .] It seems somehow rude, or cliché, or some combination of both, to tell you how much I admire your work. But it is true, so I'll say it anyway, and hope I don't embarrass you.*

Gratefully, Marta

Dear Marta, I'm so glad that you know my work and like it. If there is any other book (or books) of mine I could send along with Burdock, *would you let me know?*

All my best, Janet

20 September 2012

Dear Janet, How generous! But I think I have everything!
Open Folios *is winging its way to you.*
Thank you for taking it . . . Marta

25 September 2012

Dear Janet, Burdock *is here. It is beautiful.*
It came at a strange time. My mother is very ill, and when I look at the leaves - pristine and ravaged at once - I think of her.
She would love them, too, without making the comparison.
Thank you so much.
All my best, Marta

26 September 2012

Dear Marta, Your remarkable book has arrived, with your lovely inscription, and, again, I am so very grateful and cannot thank you enough. I am curious about the transcriptions. They look as if they were done on various old typewriters. Did you do them?
I am very sorry to hear about your mother's illness. How hard this must be for you. I send all my best wishes for her recovery. Janet

27 September 2012

Dear Janet, I'm so glad the book arrived. The transcriptions are indeed my own - and what a trial! I was working on the book so many years ago - in the early 1990s - and so the possibilities (technologically speaking) were rather limited. And, beyond this problem, far beyond it, was my great uncertainty about what an 'ideal' transcript of a Dickinson poem would look like. In the end, I decided I wanted to do a few seemingly contradictory things: call attention to the 'alienness' of the transcript - its distance, temporal and iconic, etc. - from the manuscript; show and partly enact the conflict between the regularity of type (or typesetting) and the singularity of the hand; and break down distinctions between prose and verse by insisting on following Dickinson's physical line breaks. I'm not at all sure these intentions - such as they were - translate to readers, but this was what was in my mind. And I think the spirit of Melville was working in all this too - and a story I heard about Melville insisting on always adding the punctuation to those of his works transcribed by others - his sister & wife. In transcribing Dickinson, the excessiveness of certain letters and marks fought and won over the regularizing typewriter.

And yes, initially I did do the transcriptions on typewriters. My grandfather had an amazing (if worthless!) collection of typewriters, which I commandeered for the occasion. Now I am quite sure I would proceed differently! But honestly, I still do not know exactly how. [. . .]

Thank you very much for the good thoughts about my mother. When I see her in a few weeks, I will bring Burdock to show her. I am sure she will be moved.

At the end of the book, you mention a particular way in which the original photographs were transformed. Do these photographs in the book look so very different from your originals?

I am sure you have seen Dickinson's herbarium?

I have a question about an exquisite sentence in your introduction - something about the ongoing project of decontextualization. But I will have to ask it later, since I don't have the sentence before me. When I read it, it struck me as related to the whole problem (or interest!) of the transcript, and I wanted to pursue it further.

About a year before my Father died, we took up the habit - he started it - of sending each other lists of the numbers of Dickinson poems we liked. We did not comment at all on the selections - simply exchanged them every few weeks over the course of several months. The experience was slightly uncanny, and it struck me last night that one could do such a thing with the burdock leaves. That is, that they might be exchanged as messages. The more I look at them, the more they seem to say - or at least the more I talk to myself.

Thank you so much. Marta

29 September 2012

Dear Marta, Many things in your letter - especially the mention of decontextualization - tell me that the time has come to tell you of the special reason why I wanted a copy of your book - namely, to cut some pages out of it and put them into collages. When I saw the book at Sharon Cameron's house, this desire formed itself in my mind - I began to 'see' the collages. It was the typewritten transcriptions rather than the handwritten originals that stirred my imagination. The series I want to make will also use images and charts from astronomical texts. Before starting the 'cutting' and 'scissoring' (the words leaped out of your text) of your precious only copy, I want to have your permission to do so. I will completely understand if you would prefer I not do so, and will continue my search for another copy.

The way the burdock photographs are printed makes them softer-edged and more painterly. The prints themselves are much better than the reproductions in the book. If you ever come to New York, I would be happy to show the prints to you. Some are at the Lori Bookstein Fine Art and the Davis & Langdale galleries and others are under my bed.

Your use of the word uncanny resonates with me. Doesn't it apply to our encounter?

All my best, Janet

Dear Janet, Oh but of course - cut away! I can think of no better fate for the pages of this last copy of my first book than to become collages made by your hands. And to have as company astronomical texts and charts - that is perfectly lovely. There is one - I think it's A 742 - which is very torn and cut, I wonder if you will be drawn to it . . . And another - I think A 757? - where one word 'Last' is written upside down and under other text. The word last is written in a beautiful, magnified fair-copy hand, the text that covers it is in the small, contracted hand of the working drafts. I wonder so much which ones will summon you. I only wish I had the original typescripts to send you. I moved several times since making them, and each time, things vanished, as they do. I shall search again, and if I find them, I will send them onto you - if only as curiosities.

I would love to see the burdock prints, in the galleries and under the bed, though I would not want to put you to any trouble!

As for uncanny encounters - yes - this meeting between us is as you say. And I value it all the more for the attending strangeness. There is not enough of this in correspondences - or friendships.

Gratefully, Marta

30 September 2012

Dear Marta, I am so happy that my project has your blessing, and will start work on it today. I will let you know which fragments I 'appropriate' as it's called. The book is in my studio and I am about to go out and buy fresh glue.

With many, many thanks again, Janet

During the winter, spring and summer of 2013 I made collages that yoked Marta's transcriptions of the Dickinson fragments with images I cut out of store-bought books on astronomy. I had used astronomical images in previous collages - they have great graphic clout - but something in Dickinson's words evoked the night sky. It seemed almost obligatory that images of stars and planets and moons accompany her gnomic utterances. A book called *The Transit of Venus*, 1631 to the Present, by Nick Lomb - an illustrated study of the rare astronomical event (it occurs in pairs eight years apart every hundred years) when the planet Venus crosses the disc of the sun and appears on its surface as a black circular dot - yielded a pair of spectacular black and white photographs of the sun made during the transit of 1874. I bought extra copies of the book so I could make more than two collages in which these large, mysterious orbs would figure. I also cut out a photograph of a bearded, depressed-looking man named David Peck Todd, an astronomer who was an official observer of the 1874 transit, and later of the one of 1882. Many of the Dickinson fragments read like excerpts from love letters. The consensus among scholars is that these fragments derive from drafts of letters Dickinson wrote to Judge Otis Lord, a widower with whom she is believed to have had a romantic - possibly even sexual - relationship when she was in her late forties. I had never seen a picture of Lord, and in my imagination the depressed astronomer became a kind of stand-in for him. In the collage called "No," I put Todd's picture above Dickinson's words: "Don't you know you are happiest while I withhold and not confer - don't you know that 'no' is the wildest word we consign to language?"

In the summer of 2013 I sent Marta photographs of a few collages, and was amazed to learn that the man I had connected to Dickinson in my fancy was connected to her in actuality. Marta identified him as the husband of Mabel Loomis Todd, who (with Thomas Wentworth Higginson) brought the genius of Dickinson to the attention of the larger world, by editing and publishing the hundreds of unknown poems found in the poet's house after her death in 1886. Mabel Loomis Todd is commonly referred to in Dickinson studies as the poet's "first editor," but she is remembered for another reason as well: for thirteen years she was the mistress of Dickinson's brother, Austin. The affair began in the third year of her marriage to Todd, and continued until Austin's death. No wonder the astronomer looked depressed! But, no, it appeared that Todd did not mind being cuckolded, and was even - as a close friend of Austin Dickinson and a philanderer in his own right - complicit in the affair. Mabel kept a journal in which her erotic life figured as prominently as her social and intellectual one. In *Education of the Senses*, the first volume of his series *The Bourgeois Experience, Victoria to Freud* (1984), the historian Peter Gay quotes extensively from this astonishingly un-prudish document, to make his point that the Victorians were sexual beings no less than we are. Mabel wrote about her marital and extra-marital sex life with the unembarrassed enthusiasm of a Frank Harris. She did not take up with Austin because of sexual dissatisfaction - she was the most deliciously satisfied of wives, as her journal documents over and over. Sublime sex with Austin did not replace sublime sex with David–it supplemented it.

When I made the collages, I knew nothing of this. Years ago, I had read Peter Gay's book but had not retained the name of his sex-loving diarist. That the pictures I cut out of *The Transit of Venus* could in any way be connected to Emily Dickinson's biography never crossed my mind. I wrote to Marta and said, "There does seem to be something occult going on here, and I don't think I believe in the occult." Marta wrote back: "I am thrilled to be touched by the uncanny. Like you, I have my doubts about the invisible world, but something strange and lovely may be at work. I did not know of these connections - the Dickinson/Venus transit connections - before I found them in your collages. But I assumed YOU knew." I wrote back: "What are we to make of my NOT knowing?" –Janet Malcolm, New York, November 2013

Yutaka Matsuzawa

b. 1922, Shimosuwa, Japan; d. 2006

Yutaka Matsuzawa's work bridges conceptual ideas from the West with Eastern notions of immateriality and spiritual practices involving meditation and sensory experiences. He is considered an early pioneer of conceptualism in Japan, as seen in his language-based works starting in 1961, which share many characteristics with Conceptual Art from the same period. His work infuses conceptual practices with those of Eastern and Western mysticism and spirituality, parapsychology, quantum and astrophysics, Pure Land Buddhism, and a resolute aim to transcend materiality.

Beginning in 1955 Matsuzawa spent a year residing in Wisconsin on a Fulbright Fellowship. He moved to New York City in 1956 on a Japan Society fellowship to study religious philosophy and art history at Columbia University. In New York he spent time with artists such as I. Rice Pereira, whose metaphysical ideas and writings on time and space resonated with Matsuzawa. He also became interested in the work of Robert Rauschenberg and Joseph Cornell. During this time, Matsuzawa "encountered the WOR late-night radio show, which was the source of his parapsychology and Psi."[1] A central body of the artist's work deals with "Psi powers, or cognitive abilities beyond the five senses such as precognition and clairvoyance."[2] Upon his return to Japan in March of 1957, he began to synthesize these ideas to form the basis of his own theories and practices, which he continued throughout his life.

The three works in this presentation examine several aspects of Matsuzawa's ideas and esoteric philosophy. In the oil-paint-on-paper work *Untitled* (1960–63), Matsuzawa's psi bird symbol floats enigmatically behind glowing orange brushstrokes [PL. 45]. He devised the symbol—an upside-down omega—in 1959 to represent the "liberated flight of the mind."[3] *Untitled* (1960–63), a collage of color paper, and *Untitled* (1960–63), an ink-on-paper drawing, both reference the nine-square format used in Buddhist meditation practices towards enlightenment. While the color papers in the collage [PL. 35] can be read through the Diamond World mandala, beginning in the center and descending clockwise in a spiral, in the drawing Matsuzawa has reduced the squares to a series of grids consisting of dots and pencil marks [PL. 32]. In these pieces, he invites the viewer to look beyond the physicality of the work and contemplate the cosmic wholeness.

The mysticism in Matsuzawa's work touches upon the intangible and is imbued with his radical, utopian belief system, which challenges the notion of art on every level. His work exceeds the boundaries and tenets of Conceptual Art, aiming to create space in viewers' minds for further expansion and transformation. –OS

1 Reiko Tomii, *Radicalism in the Wilderness: International Contemporaneity and 1960s Art in Japan* (Cambridge, MA: The MIT Press, 2016), 50.
2 Ibid., 52.
3 Ibid.

Elizabeth J. Milleker

b. 1935, Boston, Massachusetts

Ancient Greek mythology is often an inspiration in artist Elizabeth Milleker's practice, but her works go beyond this reference point, taking on mysterious, mythic qualities of their own. *Portal* (2010), for example, evokes a powerful entryway to the unknown, drawing one realm into another [PL. 49]. The reddish-orange glow brings to mind Japanese *torii* gates and ancient shrines dedicated to the kami Inari.

Underworld of the Brain (2010) conjures a deeply buried place where mythological patterns and the powers of ancient deities affect the psychic realm of individuals [PL. 14]. Tapping into the unexplored regions of the mind, these works are deliberately open-ended, inviting the viewer to interpret and find new meanings beyond those originally intended by the artist. –OS

Georgia O'Keeffe

b. 1887, Sun Prairie, Wisconsin; d. 1986

Georgia O'Keeffe is now one of the most well-known American artists, yet often lost is the important detail that her 1915 charcoal drawings, shown by Alfred Stieglitz at the important 291 Gallery in Manhattan, were among the first abstract artworks made by an American. More famous are her 1929 move to New Mexico (where she would remain for most of the rest of her life), her fierce independence, and her refusal to submit to the tastes of the male artists who surrounded her–none of which came easily. She faced criticism from her contemporaries for her unique artistic choices, nevertheless persisting in her use of bright colors. Her use of symmetry remains rare–even today–outside of its frequent presence in more conclusively abstract spiritual painting.

There are clues to the spirituality of her later work in her early abstract drawings, which were influenced by the teachings of her professor Arthur Wesley Dow, who encouraged his students to move beyond "topography" in landscape painting and to "express an emotion"with art.[1] Pushing this idea to its conclusion of total abstraction, the series of drawings entitled *Special* (c. 1915-17), for example, communicates internal experiences, like the intensity of the sublime, through the depiction of organic forms like water, smoke, and lightning. Though O'Keeffe resisted articulating any particular spiritual beliefs (when Allen Ginsberg asked her what she believed in, she "gestured with an open hand up and arm outstretched in a semi-circle, saying, 'It's hard to say.'"[2]), she did regularly attend services at the George Nakashima-designed monastery near her home in Abiquiu.

The three graphite drawings included in this presentation, not often on public view, were made between 45 and 55 years after these famous early pieces; the latter ones, drawn when she was losing her eyesight to macular degeneration, are sparer. The 1960s landscape, perhaps of one of the natural arches of the Southwest, resembles her paintings of the sky through holes in whitewashed bones with its gentle shading [PL. 10]. The top of the hole may be just at or above the top of the paper. The difference between the two similar 1970s drawings [PLS. 8, 9], made when she had turned her attention to painting the sky, is in the direction and evolution of the lines as they move across the page: in one, the marks all have a similar energy, heading upward and to the right, while in the other, the marks become darker and straighter as they dissipate. –**EDB**

1 Charles C. Eldredge, "Nature Symbolized: American Painting from Ryder to Hartley," in Edward Weisberger, ed., *The Spiritual in Art: Abstract Painting 1890-1985* (New York: Abbeville Press, 1986), 117.
2 Brian Nixon, "Georgia O'Keeffe and Faith," April 17, 2019, Assist News Service, https://www.assistnews.net/georgia-okeeffe-and-faith/.

Irene Rice Pereira

b. 1902, Massachusetts; d. 1971

An artistic outlier who maintained a highly individualistic abstract painting practice, I. Rice Pereira was also a poet and philosopher. Her early works were influenced by Bauhaus principles, and they integrated technology and machines with the spiritual. Pereira was interested in psychoanalysis and philosophy, and she embraced ideas put forward by Howard Hinton's *The Fourth Dimension* (1904) about the space-time continuum. She considered abstraction in three categories: representation (drawing from nature), intuition (from the subconscious), and her own variety that derived from geometric systems and symbols.

Pereira had early success in the 1930s through to the 1950s, with exhibitions at the Whitney Museum of American Art and the Museum of Modern Art. However, she was widely ignored by art critics and historians of the period. The art historian John I. H. Baur attributed this to the "path by which Pereira reached her art rather than in the nature of art itself...Her work sprang from a search for formal equivalents that would embody her inner and essentially romantic response to light, to space and the mystery of existence."[1]

Pereira's approach to abstraction and geometry was unrelated to that of Hilma af Klint, Piet Mondrian, Wassily Kandinsky, or other abstract modes of the period. Instead, in the late 1930s, she began seeking new ways to bring light into her work through the incorporation of glass, gold leaf, and other materials with reflective surfaces. *Untitled* (1934) is an abstract drawing that captures movement with an intense feminine energy [PL. 41]. There is also an "automatic drawing" aspect to this work: Pereira wrote, "The pictures makes themselves from an inner rhythm. I never plan a picture; I am simply the medium for communication."[2]

Pereira's many theories of light in relation to form and space (infinity) are widely viewed as the ruling force within her work. Indeed, she understood "light as the humanizing element that prevents man's perceptions from being frozen in their extension toward the infinity of interstellar space. It is a universally felt symbol imbedded in man's psyche."[3] Several of Pereira's writings and poems have been published, and in 1957 she self-published the artist's book *Lapis*. This volume describes her dream of the philosopher's stone with diagrams, drawings, and texts depicting her inner vision. Her art, poetry, and writings are a culmination of her philosophy and worldview that the "image of the cosmos is in the mind...and beauty nestles in the arms of the Absolute."[4] –**OS**

1 John I. H. Baur, introduction to *I. Rice Pereira*, exh. cat. (New York: Andrew Crispo Gallery, 1976), ii.
2 Ibid.
3 Ibid., iv.
4 I. Rice Pereira, *The Poetics of the Form of Space, Light and the Infinite* (New York: self-pub., 1969), 81.

Julia Phillips

b. 1985, Hamburg, Germany

In Julia Phillips's work, the body is absent, despite its centrality in her practice. Whether as a smudged and fleeting trace in *Dance Marks* (2014) [PL. 23] or implied in assembled contraptions that dictate an activity, code of conduct, or a trespassing (such as in *Bower*, *Mediator*, and *Destabilizer*), the vacuum left by the departed corporal figures across Phillips's constructions inadvertently multiplies their possible meanings, their removal a reinforcement. While many pieces have a devotional quality or inscribe a space of ritual, each also carries the suggestion of the aligned stricture that can accompany the rules governing religion, individualized asceticism, or the inherent tension in our unequal social relations.

Phillips was born and initially educated in Germany, later moving to New York for graduate school. More recently, she studied psychoanalysis at the Chicago Psychoanalytic Institute, underlining the discipline's importance within her oeuvre, which spans sculpture, works on paper, and performance. She is most known for sculptures like *Bower*, which consists of a bronze frame holding two fragile ceramic parts: one fit to a human waist and the other a cast of a forehead, together implying the arc of a bent subject. Equally, however, the mottled ceramic forehead becomes the object of devotion, held high above the sculptural base. Recently exhibited at the 2022 Venice Biennale, *Bower*'s tiled base is modeled after the sixteenth-century church of San Giorgio Maggiore, further connecting the "bow" of the body to spirituality.[1] Here the rules and order of the Catholic church are contrasted against individual belief. The earlier work *Dance Marks* presents Phillips's interest in the trail left by the body literally, in a print capturing the marks left by a dancer. Whether *Dance Marks* suggests fingerprints, like evidence, or attempts to represent an entranced individual, alone with a movement practice that borders on the spiritual, is left open. Here, the artist's interest in inward psychic experience and its material trace in the world is evident. *Dance Marks*, a monotype, was created by pouring coarse sand over a metal plate, which the artist then danced upon, leaving imprints of her activity. Cloudy yet filled with precise lines of action, the print contains two large, more concentrated gray areas, roughly separated by the width of two legs, where each foot moved. Heel prints leave emanating circular marks, and the drag of the foot is evident in scratchy lines. As the artist explained, "My work is rooted in the idea that the body is the first ground of our experiences."[2] –ECF

1 Madeline Weisburg, "Julia Phillips," La Biennale di Venezia, https://www.labiennale.org/en/art/2022/milk-dreams/julia-phillips.
2 Phoebe Collings-James, Julia Phillips, and Dr Jareh Das, "How clay is connected to our bodies," *Frieze* 223 (Fall 2021): https://www.frieze.com/article/how-clay-connected-our-bodies.

Betye Saar

b. 1926, Los Angeles, California

A pioneer of second wave feminist and postwar Black nationalist aesthetics, Betye Saar has for over fifty years consistently interwoven touchstones across time, media, faiths, and knowledge systems in her spiritually redolent and acutely political work. From prints to mixed-media assemblages, her layering of stamps, stencils, and drawings as well as her utilization of found materials, including window frames and jewelry boxes, creates pieces that are both tactile and deeply symbolic.

Born in 1926, Saar grew up in Los Angeles and Pasadena,

California. She studied design, but it was not until the mid-1960s after postgraduate coursework in printmaking that she began to create color etchings, ink drawings, and intaglio prints. Saar's practice later transitioned to her renowned assemblage work, largely inspired by a Joseph Cornell exhibition she saw in 1967 at the Pasadena Art Museum. She was drawn to Cornell's use of found objects and the otherworldliness of the boxes with their past histories and energies.

Taurus (1967)–one of Saar's early prints–incorporates intaglio with ink and watercolor, and evokes the artist's interest in cosmology in its composition and textures [PL. 24]. Several of Saar's early pieces feature astrological and mystical elements, and while *Taurus* does not use bull imagery associated with the astrological sign, it is still saturated by an "occult atmosphere" evocative of her extended explorations of spirituality, mysticism, the occult, and metaphysics.[1] These practices provide a lens through which the world can be understood as profoundly interconnected rather than singularly defined. In *Taurus,* a multiplicity of these phenomena can be inferred from the piece's astrological title, or in another possible reading, from tarot, in which *Taurus* is linked to the Hierophant, a card that stands for systems of spirituality, tradition, and knowledge. Like much of Saar's work, *Taurus* coalesces figures and symbols, offering manifold ways to explore the self and the soul. –**MH**

1 See Juvenio L. Guerra, "The Ordinary Becomes Mystical: A Conversation with Betye Saar," J. Paul Getty Trust, January 4, 2012, http://blogs.getty.edu/iris/the-ordinary-becomes-mystical-a-conversation-with-betye-saar/; Betye Saar, Jonathan Griffin, "Influences: Betye Saar," *Frieze* 182 (September 26, 2016): https://www.frieze.com/article/influences-betye-saar.

Andrei Tarkovsky

b. 1932, Zavrazh'e, Russia; d. 1986

Director Andrei Tarkovsky was born in Russia in 1932 into a literary family. He fought in World War II and was shot in the leg, which would later be amputated. After a brief itinerant period during which he studied Arabic and then worked as a metal prospector, he entered the State Institute of Cinematography to study to directing.

His film studies coincided with the Krushchev Thaw (mid-1950s through mid-1960s), a time of more freedom in the media, arts, and culture in Russia, and as a result he was able to experience selected

European and North American books, music, and films (access to outside artistic production had been previously restricted under Stalin). During this time it also became easier to make films, and Tarkovsky managed to direct several, though not without some resistance from Soviet authorities, who accused him of elitism and of having "cut [himself] off from reality."[1] He eventually left the Soviet Union, and although he never identified as a dissident, he was ardently anti-materialist. Disturbed by both the science-worship of the Communist leadership and the consumerism of the West (though he saw much Soviet art, too, as made for a kind of consumption), he worried about the destructive capacity of civilizations that had abandoned their spirituality. He wrote of Marx and Engels: "They observed the situation as it was then, without analyzing its causes: namely, man's failure to recognise that he was responsible for his own spirituality. Once man had turned history into a soulless and alienated machine, it immediately started to require human lives as the nuts and bolts that would keep it going."[2]

Included in this exhibition is a collection of clips from Tarkovksy's film *Solaris* (1972), based on Stanislaw Lem's book of the same title. The film's plot consists of scientists visiting a sentient planet whose consciousness is capable of influencing the realities of the researchers observing it, bringing forth hallucinations or apparitions of significant people and things from their pasts. The clips are of the planet's oceanic surface as depicted in the film; composed of overlapping and manipulated shots of Earth's oceans and sky, they call to mind the idea that consciousness itself may not exist solely within the bounds of the human brain. –**EDB**

1 Andrey Tarkovsky, *Sculpting in Time*, trans. Kitty Hunter-Blair (1986; rept. Austin: University of Texas Press, 1987), 165.
2 Ibid., 235.

Lenore Tawney

b. 1907, Lorain, Ohio; d. 2007

The space around Lenore Tawney's work–the air and light circling the towering "woven forms" for which she is best known, the expanse of her studio, the meticulous zone of graph paper–is a material that the artist utilized as much as linen, wool, ink, or paper. Tawney is a pioneer of fiber art, only achieving recognition later in her life for works that bent weaving into a fine art and thread into three dimensions. Her work, in a sense, is rooted in drawing: the thread a new kind of line. In the late 1940s she studied at the Institute of Design in Chicago (the "New Bauhaus") where Laszlo Moholy-Nagy, she remembered, "taught me to draw, when I thought I could not draw."[1] Tawney turned to weaving in the mid 1950s, beginning a decades-long study of traditional techniques ranging from tapestry to Peruvian gauze weaving. Out of the strictures of folk and traditional craft, Tawney developed new methods and forms that operated both within and against the weave's grid, a relationship she would continue in her drawing, collage, and free-form fiber works in the later 1960s.

In 1957 Tawney moved to the Coenties Slip, a former maritime industrial area at the tip of Manhattan. There she found herself in a cohort of artists–among them Agnes Martin, Ellsworth Kelly, and Robert Indiana–taking refuge from nearby Abstract Expressionism. All Minimalists, many of the Coenties artists worked with the grid, and with it they explored infinite dimensions of color and gradient, generating volume (through thread or on a flat canvas) where there was none. Like many engaged in minimal form at this moment, Tawney turned to Eastern religion– Indian spiritualism and Zen Buddhism–as well as Western thinkers like Carl Jung to locate a ritualistic undercurrent for the production of her work and a notion of universal transcendence that could connect her shapes to a sense of metaphysical being. In 1964, Tawney began a series of drawings on graph paper initially inspired by her studies of the Jacquard loom, a nineteenth-century patent that enabled the mass manufacture of woven design; *Eclipse* (1965) [PL. 30] and *Untitled* (1965) [PL. 31] are part of this group. The artist mirrored the collision between intricate form and commercial repetition in her drawings, which begin to depart two dimensions. Indeed, in the 1990s Tawney would reinterpret them as hanging sculptures in a series titled *Drawings in Air*.[2] –**ECF**

1 Erin Alexa Freedman, "Questions about Lenore Tawney: An Interview with Kathleen Nugent Mangan," *Bauhaus Imaginista* 2, https://www.bauhaus-imaginista.org/articles/4170/questions-about-lenoretawney?0bbf55ceffc3073699d40c945ada9faf=2ada1d1b892c42c58236b0351a31d12c.

2 "Ink Drawings," from the website of the Lenore G. Tawney Foundation, https://lenoretawney.org/lenore-tawney/work/drawing/.

Warlimpirrnga Tjapaltjarri

b. circa 1950s

Tjapaltjarri is Pinupti, an Indigenous Australian group from the territory in the Gibson and Great Sandy regions of Western Australia. Until the artist was in his twenties, he led a semi-nomadic life in the remote regions of this desert. Tjapaltjarri's family is often referred to as the "Pinupti Nine," a group thought to be the last existing Pinupti nomads. In the 1950s and '60s, the British government began to forcibly relocate many Pinupti people into settlements in order to conduct Blue Streak Missile tests in the Western Desert. Tjapaltjarri's family resided in an area so secluded that they were overlooked and continued to live itinerantly until a chance encounter in 1984 with residents of Kiwirrkurra.[1] Tjapaltjarri now lives between Kiwirrkurra and Kintore.

International recognition of Tjapaltjarri's work coincided with the burgeoning Desert Painting and Papunya Tula Art Movement of the early 1970s.[2] Papuyna Tula is an artist cooperative that began in 1971 when the encouragement of a schoolteacher inspired a group of Indigenous men to paint a blank school wall in the Papuyna settlement, which is located in the Western Desert and home to predominantly Luritja/Pintupi language groups.[3] Indigenous Australian art gained further visibility in the United States following a highly successful 1988 show at the Asia Society called *Dreamings: The Art of Aboriginal Australia*.[4]

Tjapaltjarri's canvasses cite ceremonial painting, sand drawing, and the ornamentation of bodies, using dots, bold lines, and circles to create elaborate abstract patterns. There is a simultaneous exposition and concealment of sacred symbols in the meandering lines of his compositions, which in the work *Maruwa* (2017) resemble topographical lines, fingerprints, or the interior rings of a tree trunk [PL. 39]. This enveloping sense of time and memory is echoed in the twisting lines of Tjapaltjarri's paintings, which immerse viewers in a visual field that seems to morph before their very eyes and which encourage a ritual in the form of deep, meditative looking. –**MH**

1 Alana Mahoney, "The day the Pinupti Nine entered the modern world," BBC News, December 23, 2014, https://www.bbc.com/news/magazine-30500591.

2 Two of Tjapaltjarri's brothers, Walala and Thomas, have also gained international recognition as artists.

3 The collective officially formed in 1972 and today has 49 shareholders and represents around 120 artists. "History," the website of Papuyuna Tula Artists, Pty. Ltd., https://papunyatula.com.au/history//; Luke Scholes, "Land, loss and identity: art of a great Pinupti lineage," The National Gallery of Victoria, *Art Journal* 50, January 2, 2013, https://www.ngv.vic.gov.au/essay/land-loss-and-identity-art-of-a-great-pintupi-lineage/; "Papunya Tula," the website of the National Museum Australia, August 5, 2022, https://www.nma.gov.au/defining-moments/resources/papunya-tula.

4 Lucia Colombari, "1988: The Scintillating Arrival of Aboriginal Australian Art in the U.S.," in *Beyond Dreamings: The Rise of Indigenous Australian Art in the United States*, exh. cat., ed. Henry F. Skerritt (Charlottesville, VA: Kluge-Ruhe Aboriginal Art Collection, University of Virginia, 2019), 9, https://kluge-ruhe.org/wp-content/uploads/2019/02/12_Kluge-Ruhe_BeyondDreamingsCatalog_Feb2019_Lo.pdf.

Unknown artist

c. 18th–19th century, Rajasthan, India

Yantras are important meditative and protective diagrammatic guides, either drawn on paper or engraved in metal, representative of a deity. The origin of yantras has ties to Hinduism, Jainism, and Buddhism, and is believed to date back to 11,000-10,000 BCE. These works are often created by the practitioner to aid with meditation. In Sanskrit, Sarvatobhadra translates to "auspicious, or guarded, on all sides," and Sarvatobhadra yantras are typically composed of carefully balanced lines, squares, and shapes that reflect the abstracted visual characteristics of the deity. The yantra in this presentation reflects this symmetry with an equal number of squares on each side [PL. 33]. A yantra is created beginning with a central point (Bindu means "point" or "dot" in Sanskrit) and radiating out. The Bindu is viewed as the cosmic origin and a symbol representing the universe. –OS

Unknown Shaker artist

19th century, New York

At the height of its membership, the Shaker community experienced an expansion in sensibility borne of a crisis of meaning: changing attitudes among the youthful members had begun to provoke concern among the older Shakers that the community faced impending attrition and decline. When in 1837 a fourteen year-old girl at Watervliet, NY (the first settlement founded by Shaker leader Mother Ann Lee when she left Britain for the New World) had a series of spiritual visions in which she established contact with early Shaker Believers and with Christ himself, it ushered in a brief flowering of visitations from saints, religious figures, angels, deceased former slaves, and "native spirits." These visions were, at least initially, encouraged by the Central Ministry at New Lebanon as a revival of religiosity, and the period came to be known as "Mother Ann's Work" or the "Era of Manifestations."

The "gifts," as they were called, first appeared as shaking, dancing, and glossolalia. So many "native spirits" visited the young Shaker women, speaking through their instruments in broken English about the sorrows inflicted upon them by the white man, that the elders decided to conduct several farewell ceremonies before they finally succeeded in ushering the spirits back to whence they came. The Central Ministry eventually issued a decree that only Shakers eighteen and older could be vessels and that gifts had to be written down for the elders before being shared with the community as a whole. Whether or not this was indeed an attempt to "exclude the bodies"[1] of youthful instruments and to render the threateningly physical gifts of the late 1830s into benign text and song, it resulted in a shift toward the production of art. Nearly all of the 200 extant Shaker gift drawings were produced in New Lebanon and nearby Hancock between the years of 1843 and 1856.

This particular unattributed 1843 work dates from among the earliest gift drawings, many of them called "sacred sheets" or "sacred rolls" [PL. 20]. Perhaps as a result of the decree to put visions into text, most of the early drawings have a distinctly lexigraphical quality and are abstract, resembling calligraphy in their lack of iconography. Drawing may also have been less familiar to people raised in Shaker iconoclasm, or it may simply be that mystical art often takes abstract form. Some early works include simple drawings of tomahawks, snakes, birds, and plants, but they usually comprise two approaches to "spirit writing": letters from the Latin alphabet assembled into unfamiliar words and phrases or even scattered across the page in composition and asemic writing that contains no recognizable characters. Over time, the gift drawings became more colorful and iconographic, incorporating watercolor and cutwork in their depictions of fruits, vessels, and even historical figures, before their production abruptly stopped and the drawings were put into storage, not to be rediscovered until the 1930s. It seems likely that some were destroyed.

In this piece, on the recto side, lines drawn by ruler, sun- or flower-like drawings, and a combination of English and asemic writing fill a classically Shaker symmetrical arrangement of circles and semi-circles probably drawn by compass. On both recto and verso, the characters progress from legible to abstract to highly ornamented and back again, dissolving or exploding into clouds of dots, flowers arranged into sentences, groupings of lines that traverse the nested semi-circles: a communication of the transmutability of literal and abstract meaning and of the possibility of otherworldly information penetrating to this material plane. –**EDB**

1 Martha Ellen Stortz, "From Bodies to Brooms: Resistance to Routinization in the Shaker Era of Manifestations," *Journal of Ritual Studies* 12, no. 1 (Summer 1998): 9-16.

Bernadette Van-Huy

b. Queens, New York

In Bernadette Van-Huy's *Home Improvements* (2019) an off-kilter letter "O," like one might find in storefront signage, floats in from the bottom edge and converges with large, planetary spheres [PL. 21]. Within this suspended environment, small musical notes appear stranded from the musical staff or located high above it; one cluster of notes bends at an angle, suggesting a dangling mobile or model of a solar system. The drawing evokes both exponential depth and an airy, distant headspace. This enigmatic thought-world is echoed in *Spinning with Spinoza* (2019), in which we see a pile of sandbags that are turned upright and seem to hop or twirl [PL. 22]. These simple means of weighing things down are here given balletic lightness and animism. On the sides of four of these bags appears some more musical notes, within which the existential question "WHAT'S MY WORTH?" is spelled out.

Both drawings were part of Van-Huy's 2019 exhibition at Svetlana Gallery in New York, during which actual sandbags were placed around the gallery floor and prints on Plexiglas sheets recounted fragments of a fictional character's inner dialogue. In these works and in her other projects, Van-Huy tends to inhabit cultural forms or artistic media at a provocative remove, loosening their conventional codes. This has ranged from her collaborative work with Bernadette Corporation since the 1990s in fashion, styling, photography, and the authoring of novels and long-form poetry to her recent solo endeavors. –**AO**

Jack Whitten

b. 1939, Bessemer, Alabama; d. 2018

Throughout his over-fifty-year career, Jack Whitten pushed the material processes of painting, printmaking, drawing, and sculpture in a continual pursuit of abstract art that condenses and conveys contemplation, spiritual knowledge, or a religious feeling. The frequent use of a black-and-white color palette in Whitten's work also has political significance, as Whitten was a child of the segregated American South who came of age during the height of 1960s civil rights struggles. But in his works, this black-and-white palette rarely settles into a simple either/or, instead developing into a complex spectrum of grays and moiré patterns that oscillate between hues.[1]

The frottage procedure was something that Whitten began investigating in the early 1970s. With his canvases on the floor of his studio, sometimes with objects arranged underneath, he layered colors of acrylic paint and then dragged a tool or long striated edge across the surface to reveal mixes of colors, incidents, and forms. In his later series of *Radiator Drawings* (2010) Whitten used a similar rubbing process on rice paper, producing a specter-like indexical effect. In *Radiator Drawing #5* (2010) a music of the spheres emerges–a dynamic, cosmic relation [PL. 28]. The vertical striations give the sense of a data image beamed in from elsewhere (as in a radar screen), while the perfect circles with intersecting lines between them suggest interplanetary connectivity. The series takes its name from the car part that Whitten repurposed as a drawing tool in order to make these works. Of this series, Whitten wrote in 2015: "The machined pattern of the grill juxtaposed with the play of gestural mark making transcends 'science vs. nature' into a symbol of sensuality."[2] –**AO**

1 Jack Whitten, interview by Jarrett Earnest, *The Brooklyn Rail*, February 2017, https://brooklynrail.org/2017/02/art/JACK-WHITTEN-with-Jarrett-Earnest.

2 Jack Whitten, unpublished writings, January 2015.

Cici Wu

b. 1989, Beijing

In 2000, a fifteen-year-old autistic boy named Yu Man-hon ran away from his mother at a train station on Hong Kong's Kowloon peninsula, sixteen miles from the border of Shenzen province in mainland China. Somehow, hours later, he crossed the border, without identification and with a diagnosed mental age of two. Without a passport, he was shuttled between immigration authorities and ultimately callously let go, both sets of authorities abdicating their duty of care. He was never seen again. The episode captivated public attention in China and came to symbolize the tension between the mainland and Hong Kong. In Hong Kong, which had just passed to Chinese rule in 1997, people worried about how the shift would impact everyday life; mass protests against growing Chinese totalitarianism and dictatorship have continued repeatedly since 1997. On the other hand, in Shenzen province, Hong Kong was seen as wealthy and insulated.[1] The artist Cici Wu, an immigrant from Beijing growing up in Hong Kong, was eleven when Yu Man-hon went missing–old enough to know the simultaneous intimacy and separation between Hong Kong and mainland China. In her piece on Yu Man-hon, she resuscitates the boy himself from the moral and political tale his disappearance had become.

Wu's work spans sculpture, installation, performance, video, and many other visual means. Rather than medium specificity, Wu's works share an interest in themes of collective memory, multidimensional time, and histories of affect and emotion. *The Unfinished Return of Yu Man-hon* (2019) is a film surrounded by an installation of found and carefully wrought objects, mostly made of paper.[2] In the film, the figure of Yu Man-hon is seen wandering through different sites–on a ferry, in a marketplace, at a bus depot. Whether these scenes imagine the boy's days after his disappearance or conjure a enlightened celestial being is left indeterminate.[3] The ritual space of the installation is strewn with offerings: paper lanterns, glowing lamps, and small animal sculptures. Among these are also works on paper like *The Disappearance of Yu Man-hon (storyboard 02)* (2017), printed with the word "wind" in small letters (other *storyboard* works feature words like "hope" and "justice") [PL. 34]. These sheets of paper recall joss offerings, used in ancestral worship to send the spirit to another dimension and afterlife. They align Yu Man-hon with the natural elements (wind), granting him elemental power and presenting ritualized harmony and peace as the true horizon of justice for his case. –**ECF**

1 Carol A. G. Jones, ed., "The Disappearance of Yu Man-hon," in *Lost in China?: Law, Culture and Identity in Post-1997 Hong Kong*, Cambridge Studies in Law and Society (Cambridge: Cambridge University Press, 2015), 114–40.

2 Billy Tang, "Poetic Justice for Yu Man-hon: Cici Wu," *Mousse*, October 13, 2010, https://www.moussemagazine.it/magazine/cici-wu-billy-tang-2020/.

3 In the press release for this project and exhibition, Wu specificied that the film constructed a non-ghostly perspective.

Plates

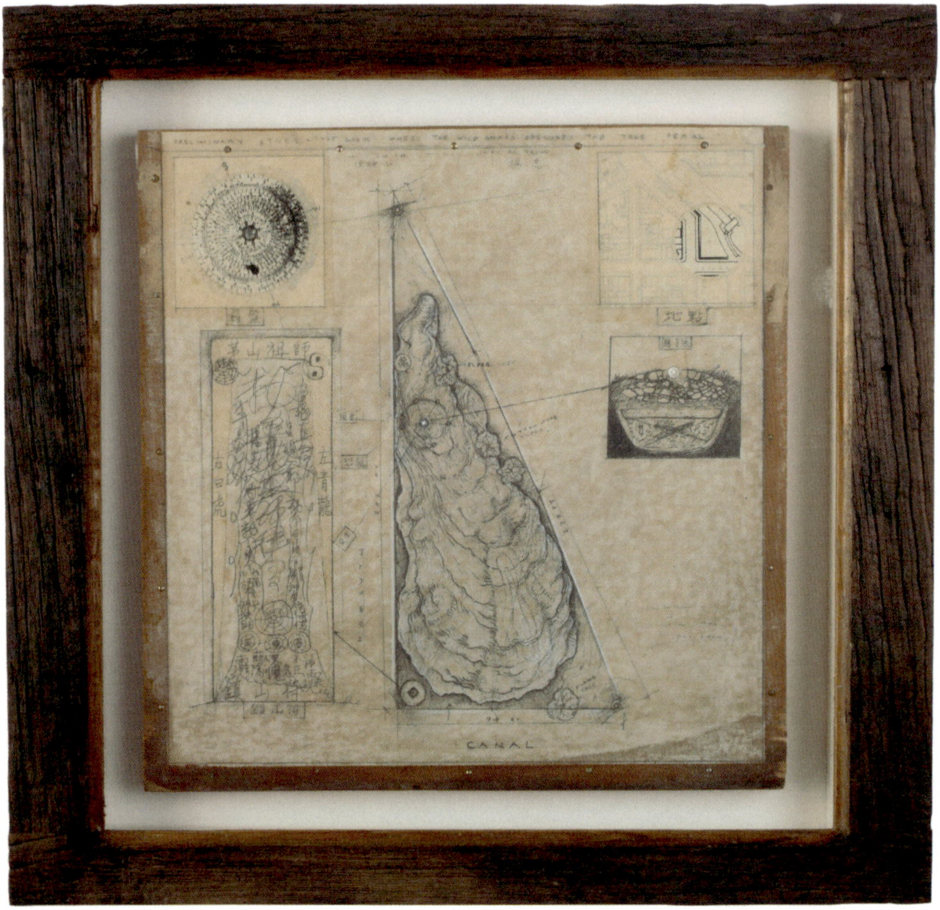

PL. 1 Mel Chin, *Garden where the Wild Grass Obscures the True Pearl, 1987*

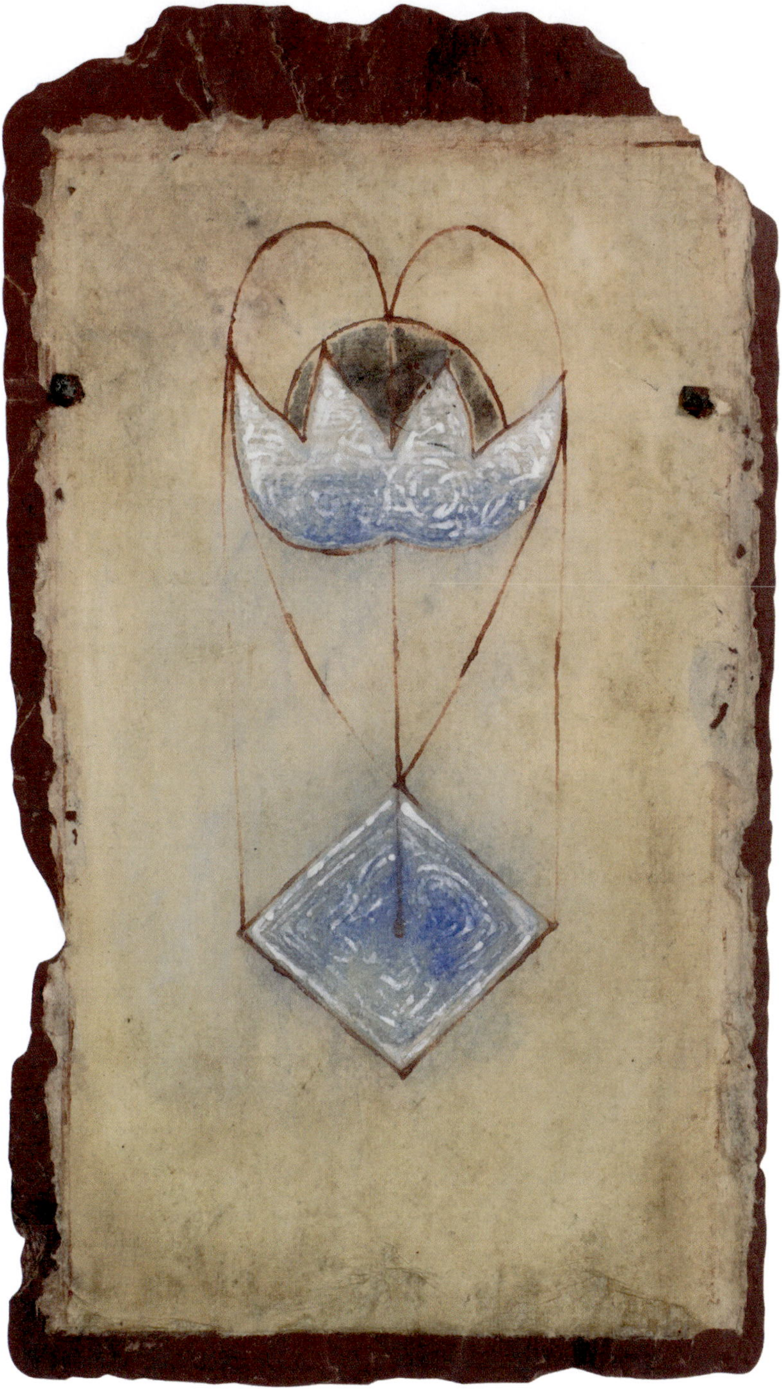

PL. 2 Mel Chin, *Tantric Dream Diagram*, 1991

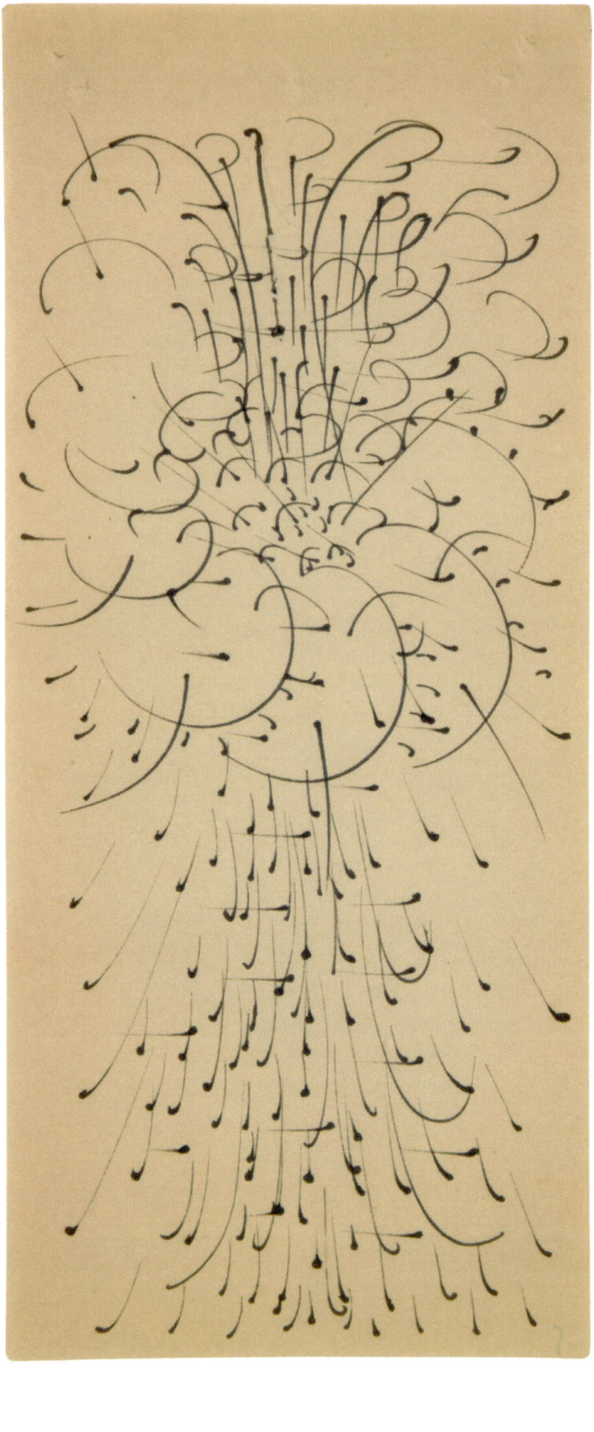

PL. 3 Jordan Belson, *Peacock Book Drawing 07*, 1952

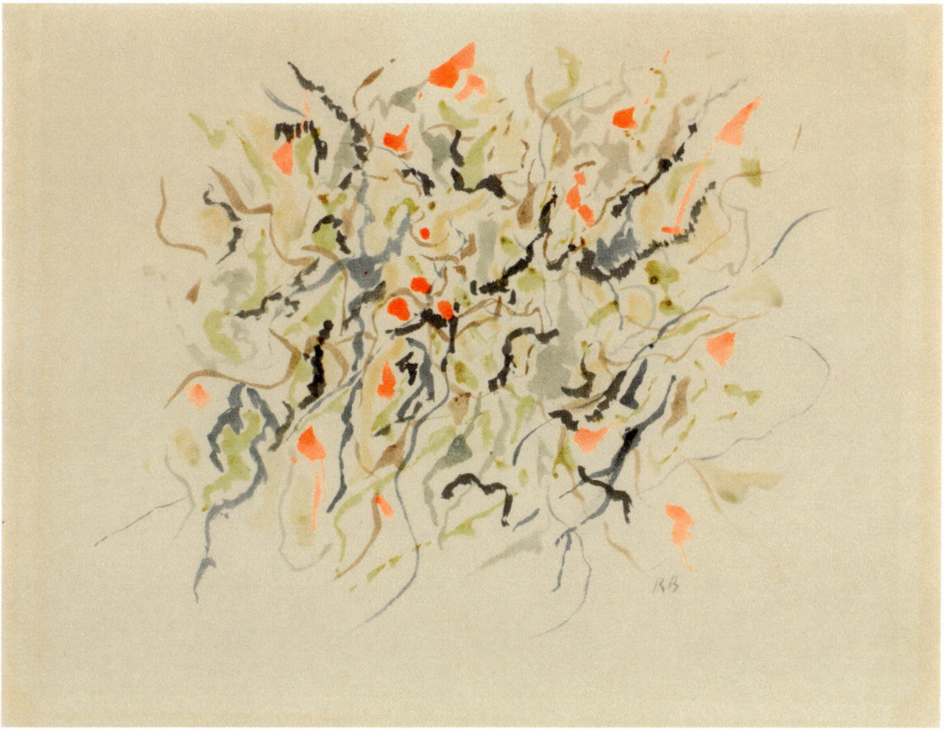

PL. 4 Roland Barthes, *Sans Titre-22 Octobre 1973*, 1973

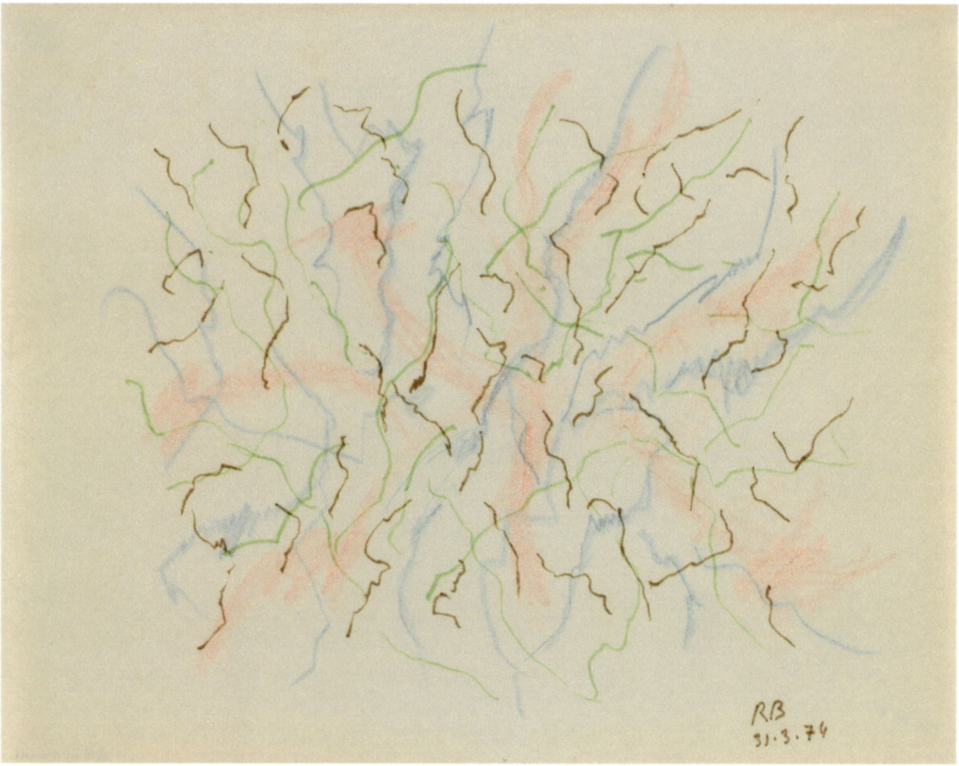

PL. 5 Roland Barthes, *Sans Titre-31 Mars 1974*, 1974

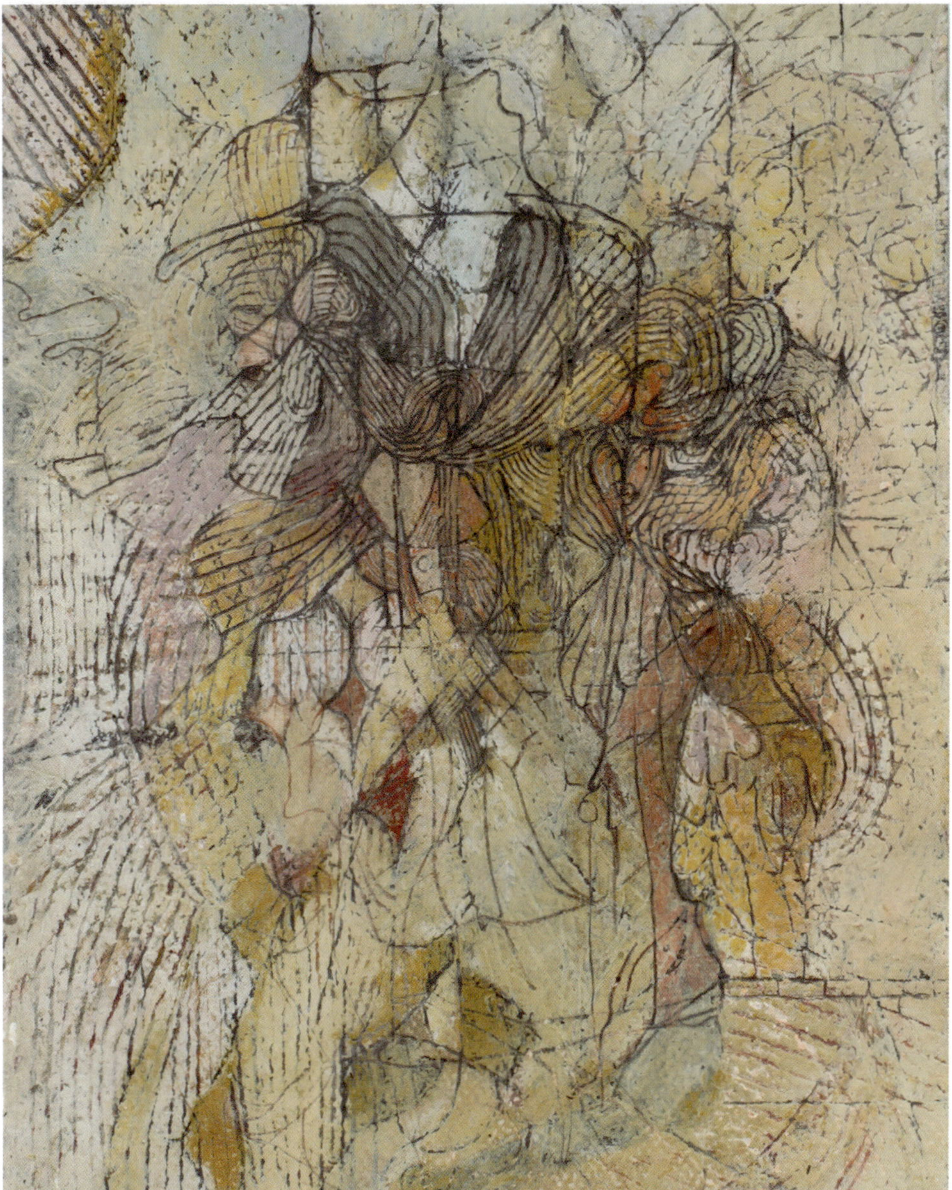

PL. 6 Robert Bittenbender, *Saturina*, 2018

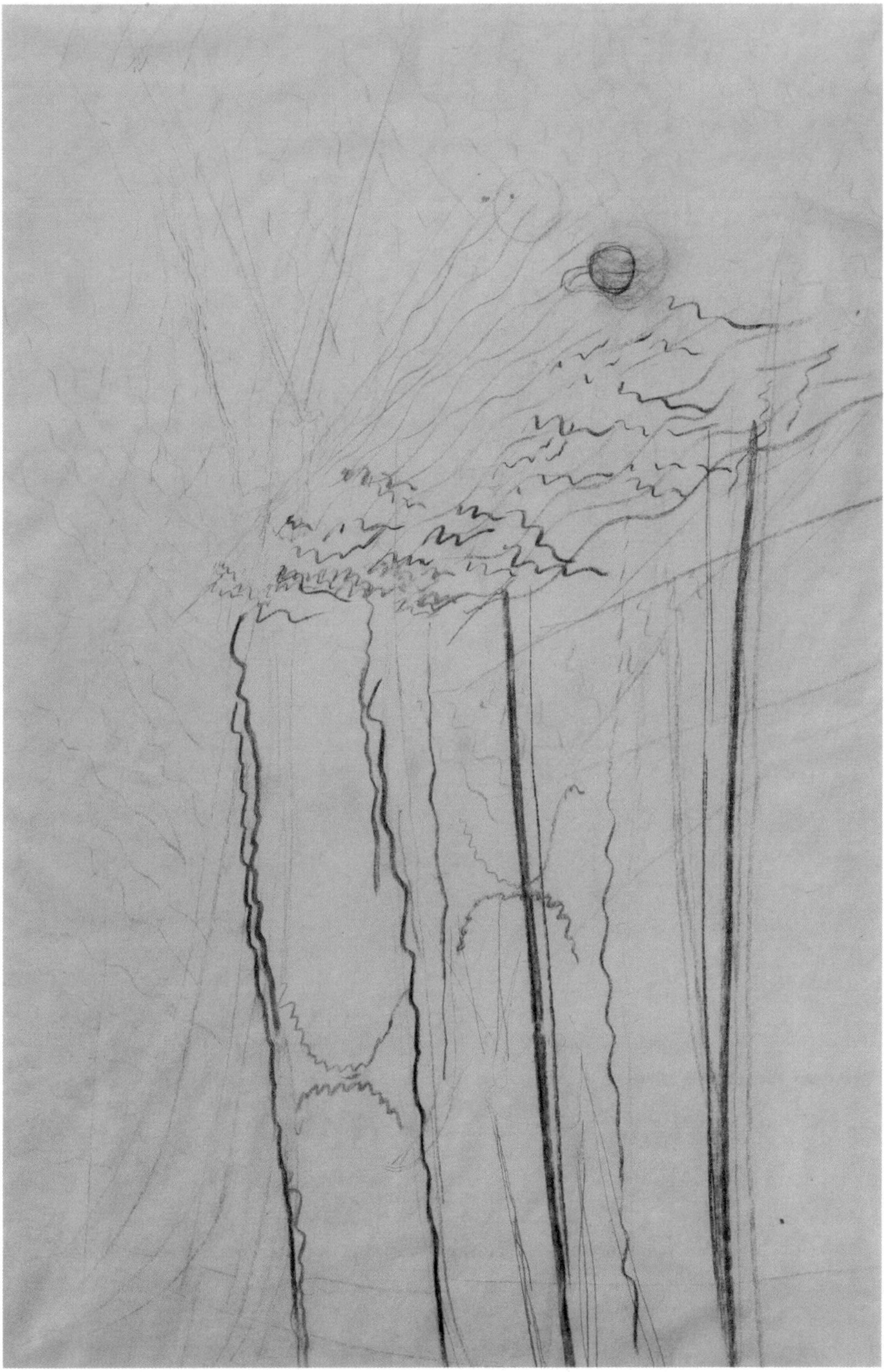

PL. 7 Ilka Gedő, *Untitled (table #2)*, 1949

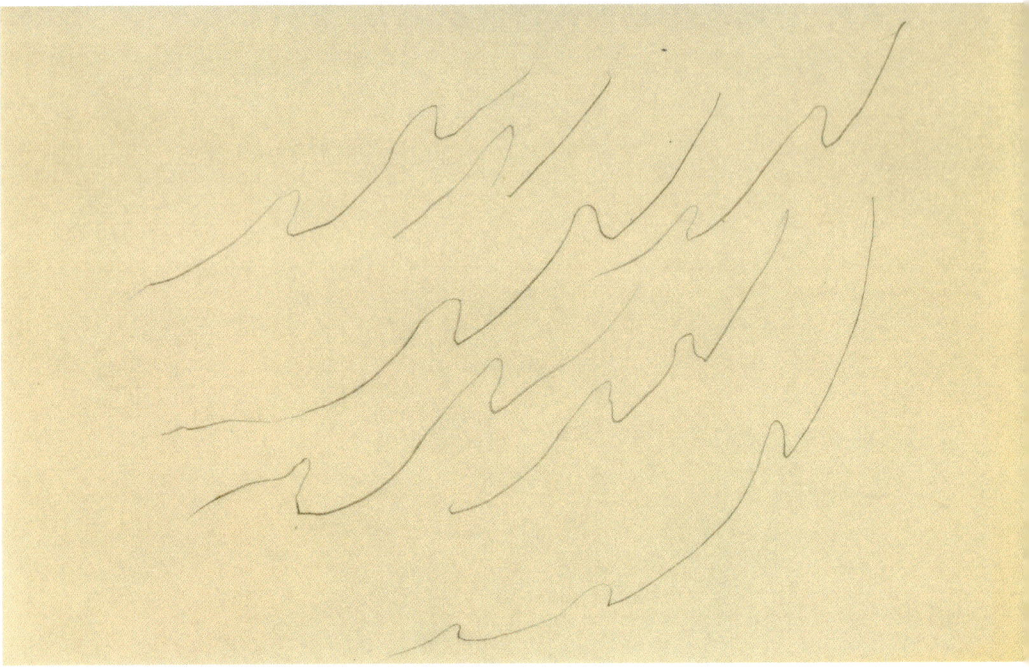

PL. 8 Georgia O'Keeffe, *Untitled (Abstraction)*, 1970s

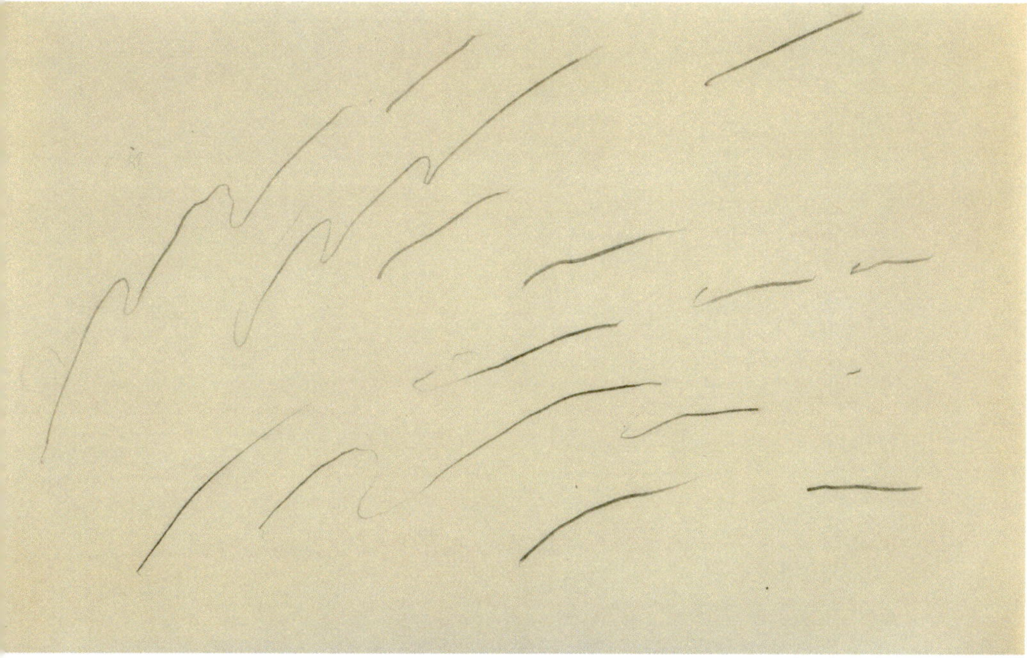

PL. 9 Georgia O'Keeffe, *Untitled (Abstraction)*, 1970s

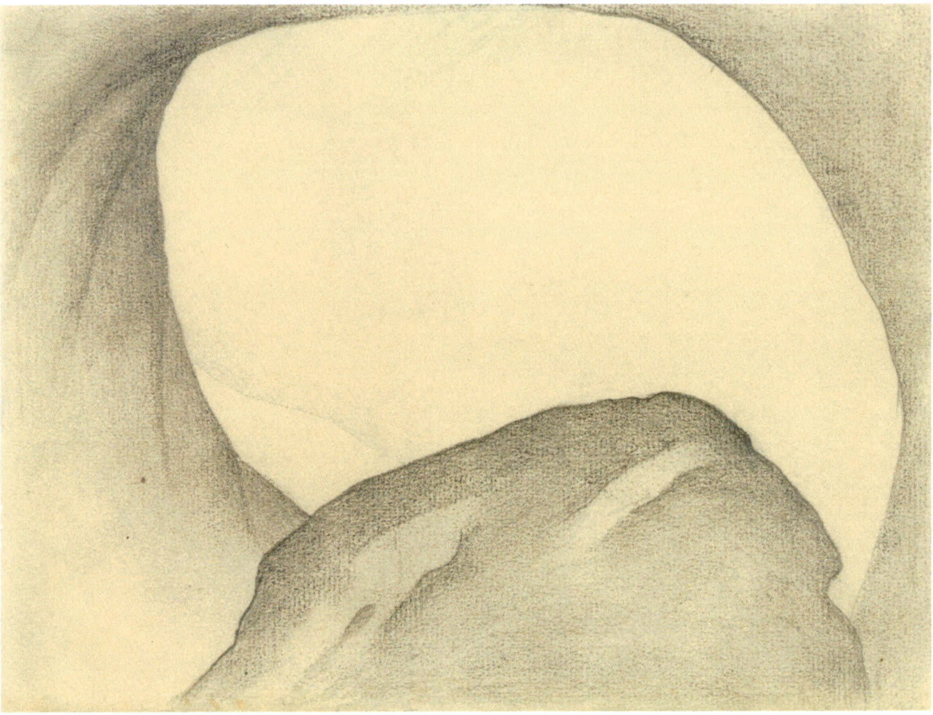

PL. 10 Georgia O'Keeffe, *Untitled (Landscape)*, 1960s

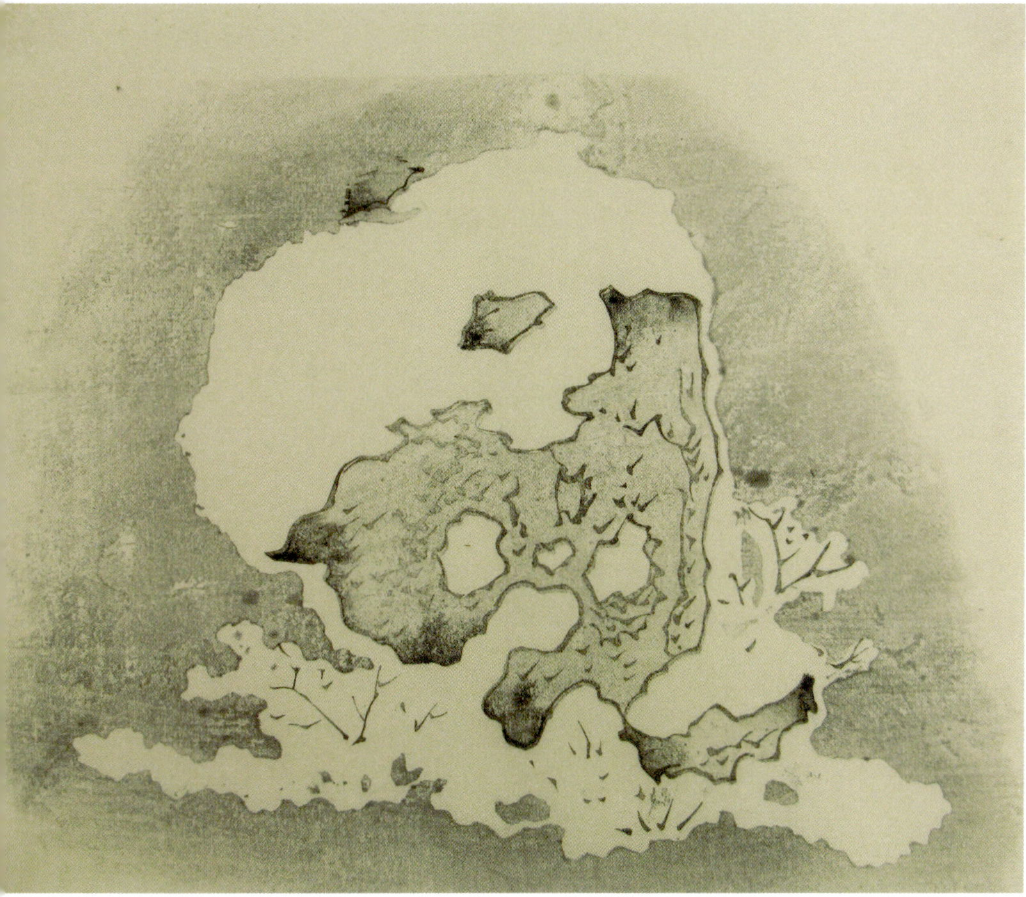

PL. 11 Hu Zhengyan, Illustration from the *Ten Bamboo Studio Manual of Calligraphy and Painting* (*Shizhuzhai shuhua pu*), 1679–1870

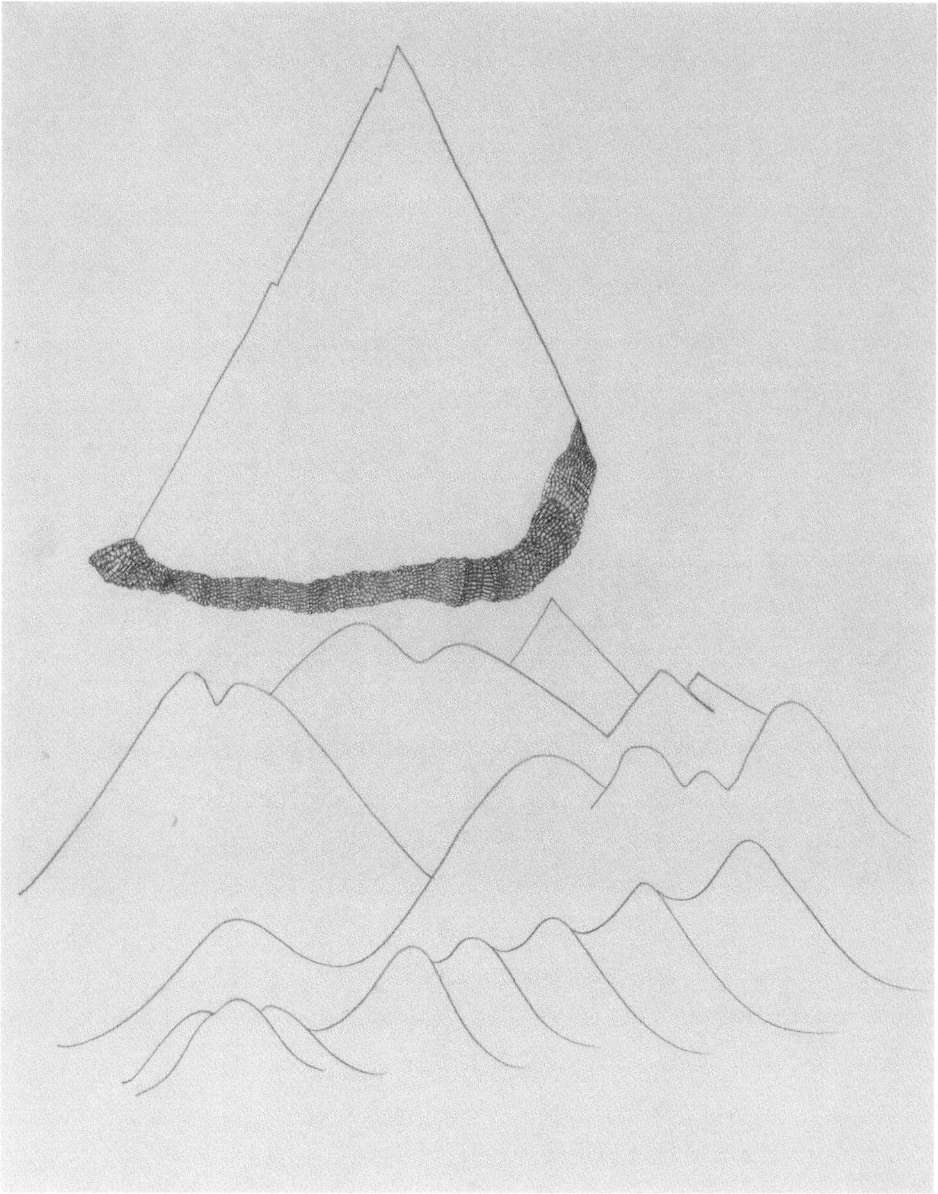

PL. 12 Walter De Maria, *Floating Mountain*, c. 1961–64

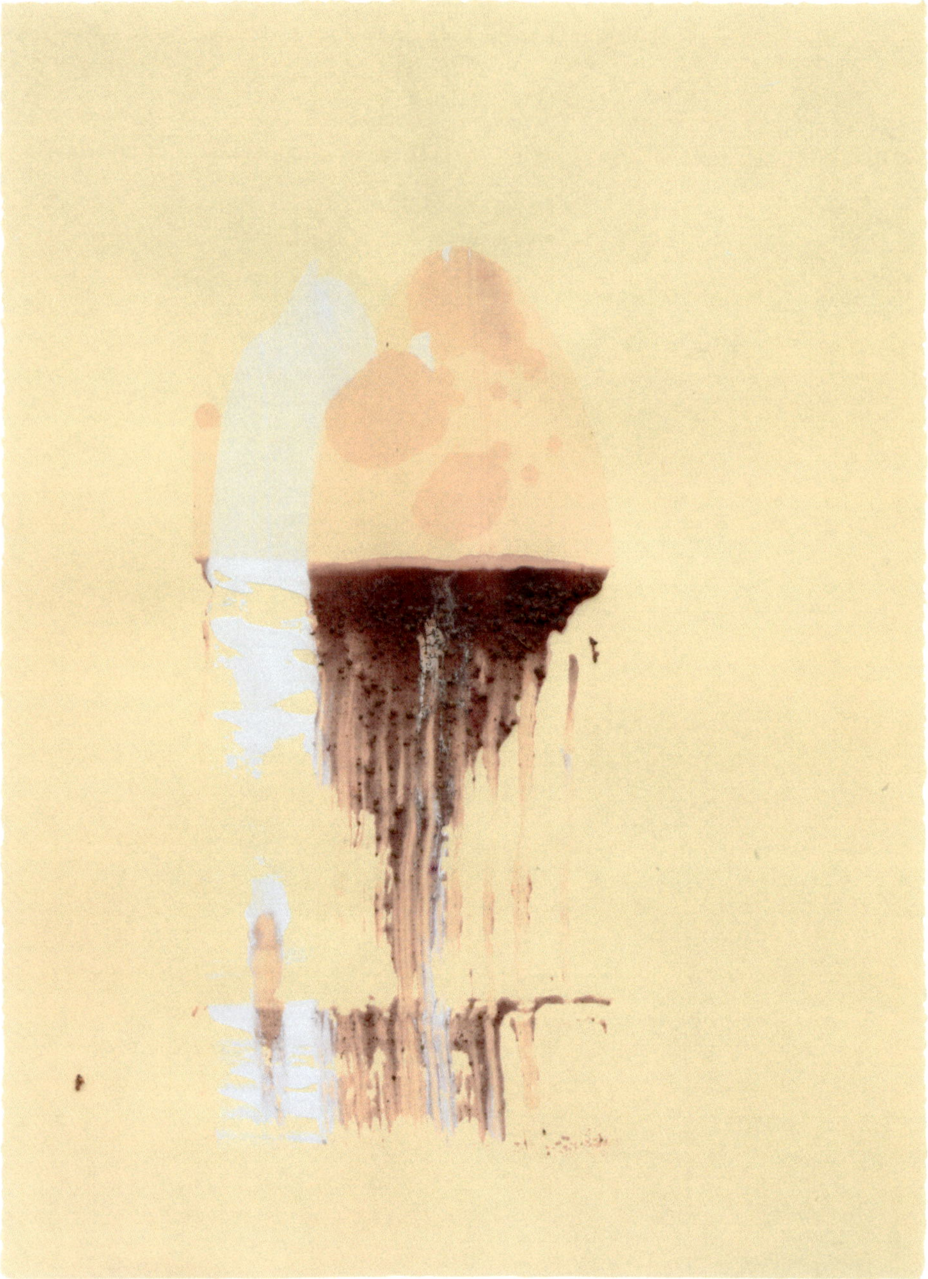

PL. 13 Duane Linklater, *break up swept up all of the willows 1*, 2022

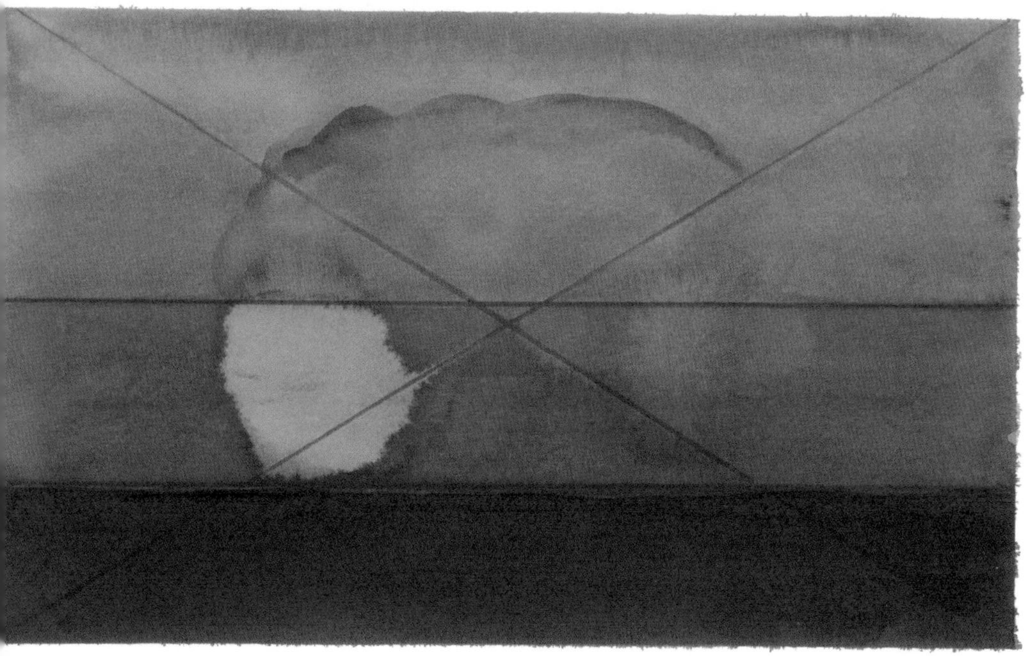

PL. 14 Elizabeth Milleker, *Underworld of the Brain*, 2010

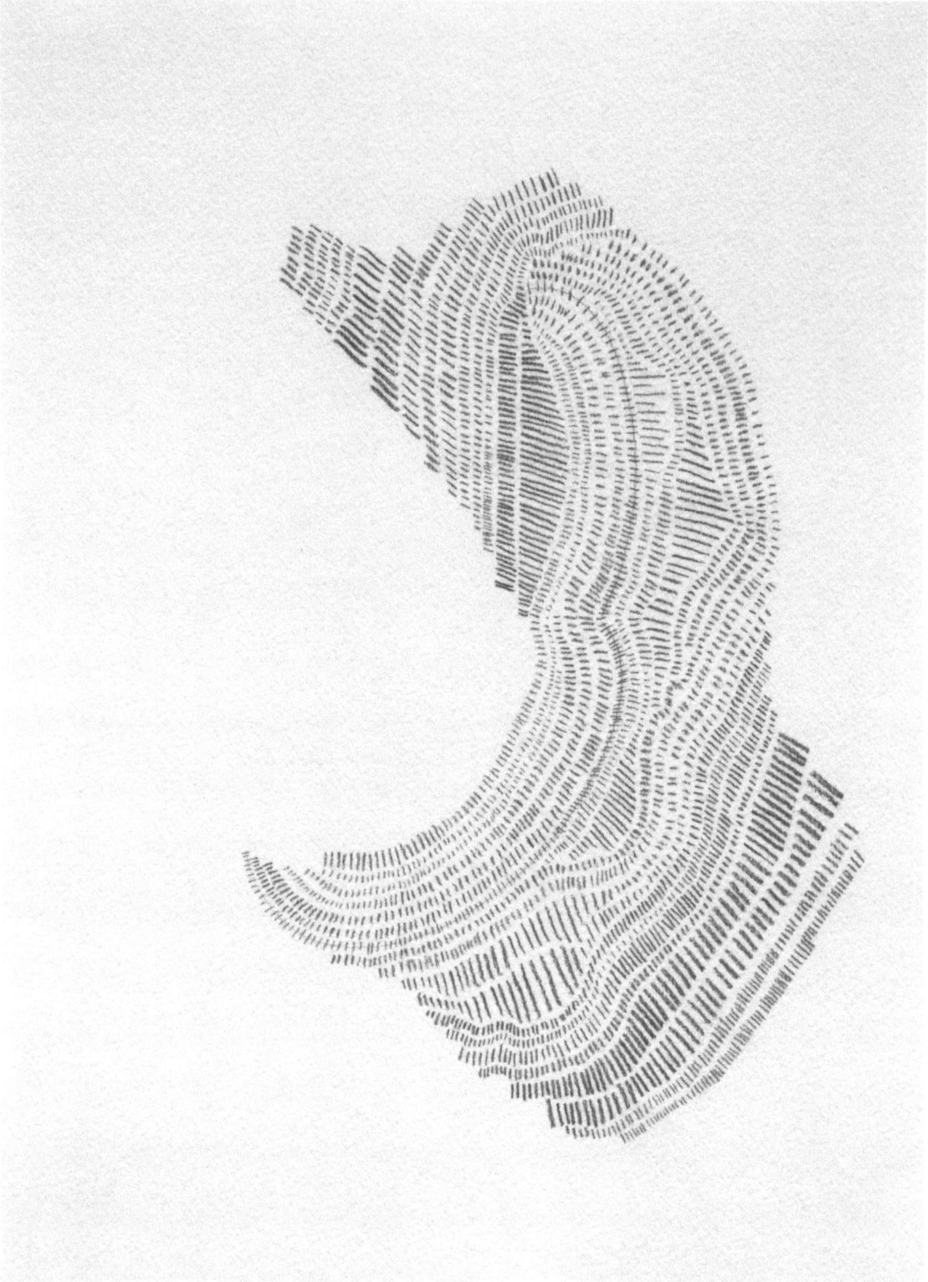

PL. 15 Duane Linklater, *Migraine 2*, 2022

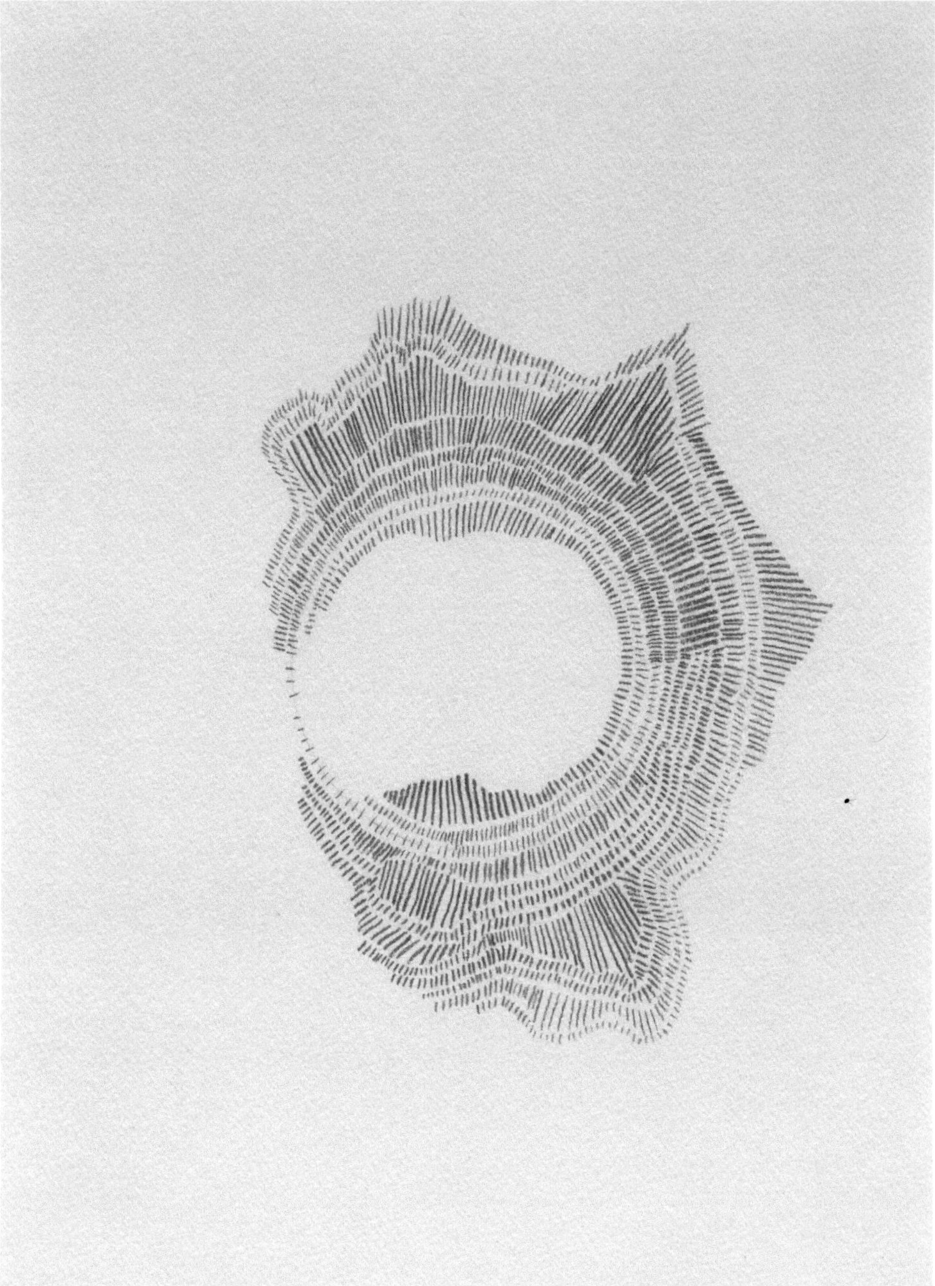

PL. 16 Duane Linklater, *Migraine 1*, 2022

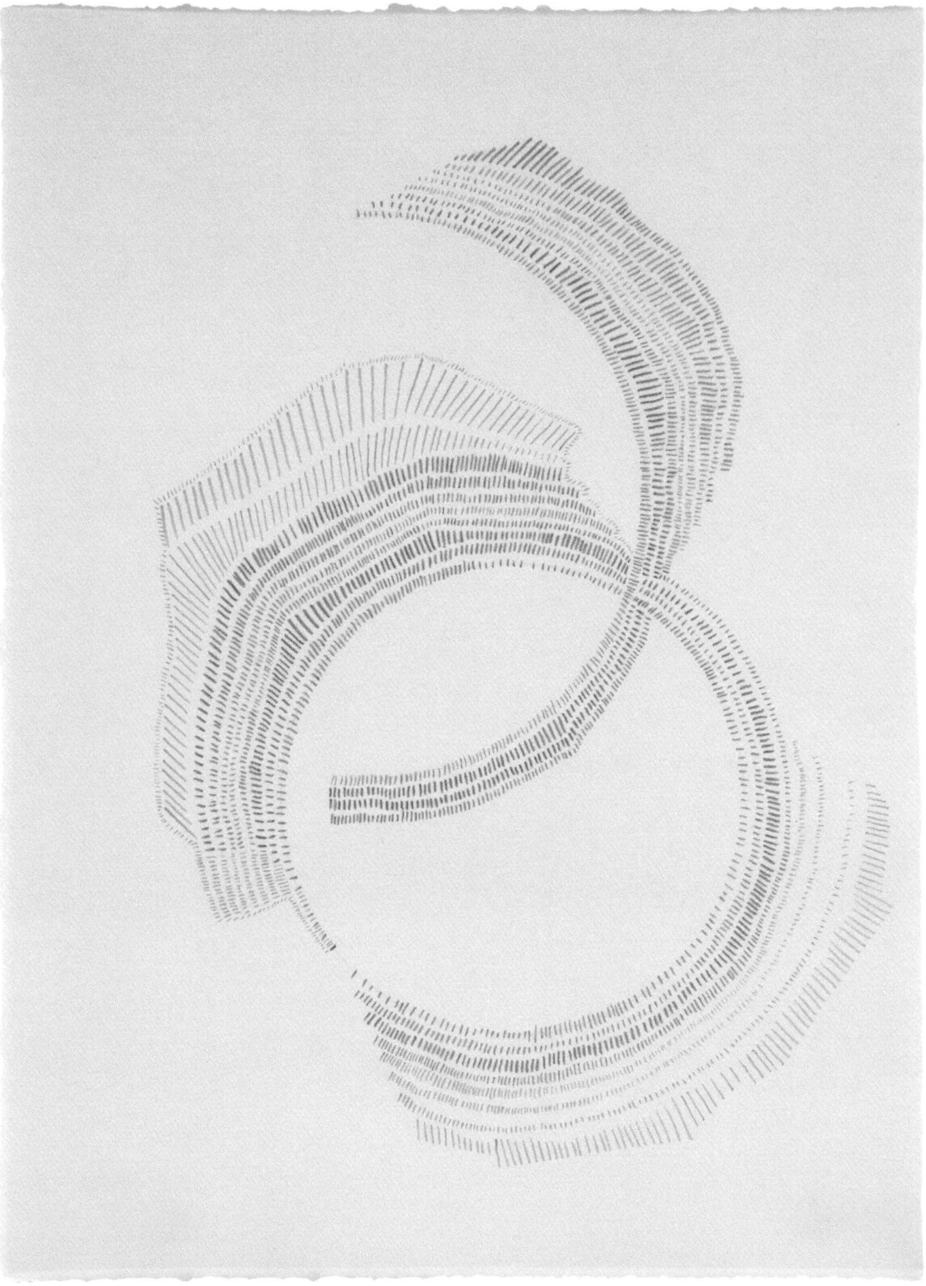

PL. 17 Duane Linklater, *Migraine 3*, 2022

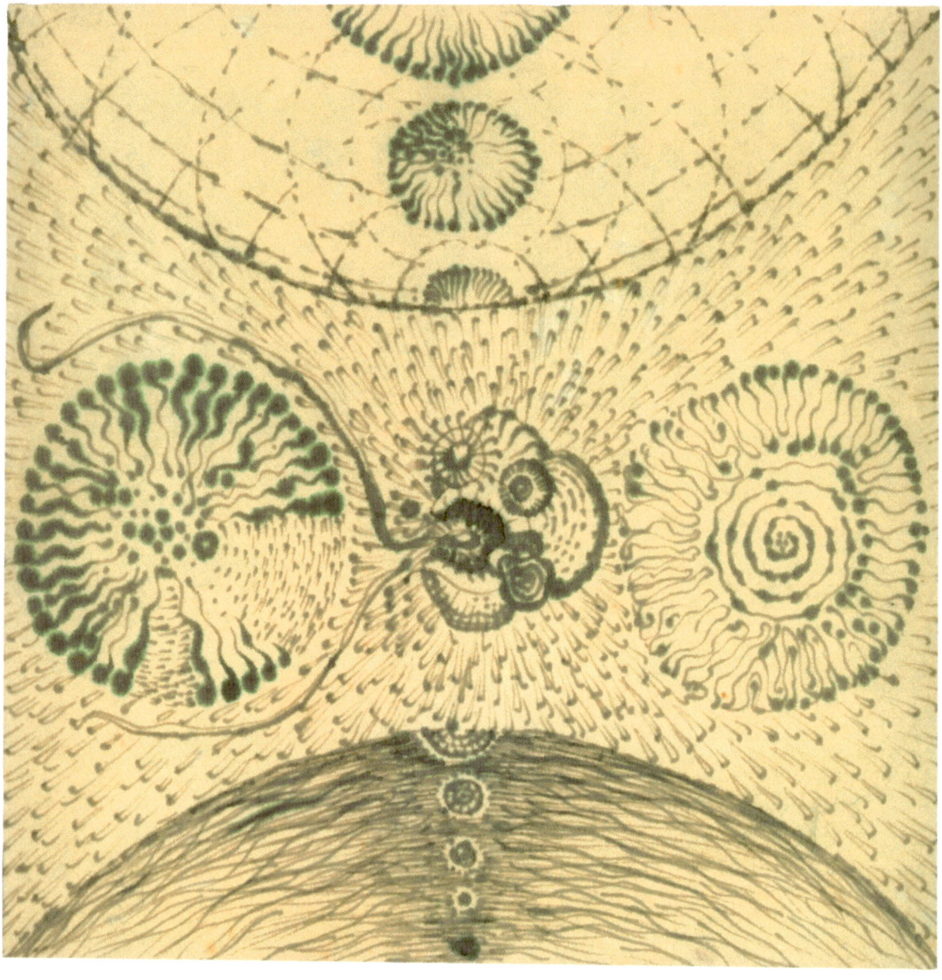

PL. 18 Jordan Belson, *Brain Drawing*, 1952

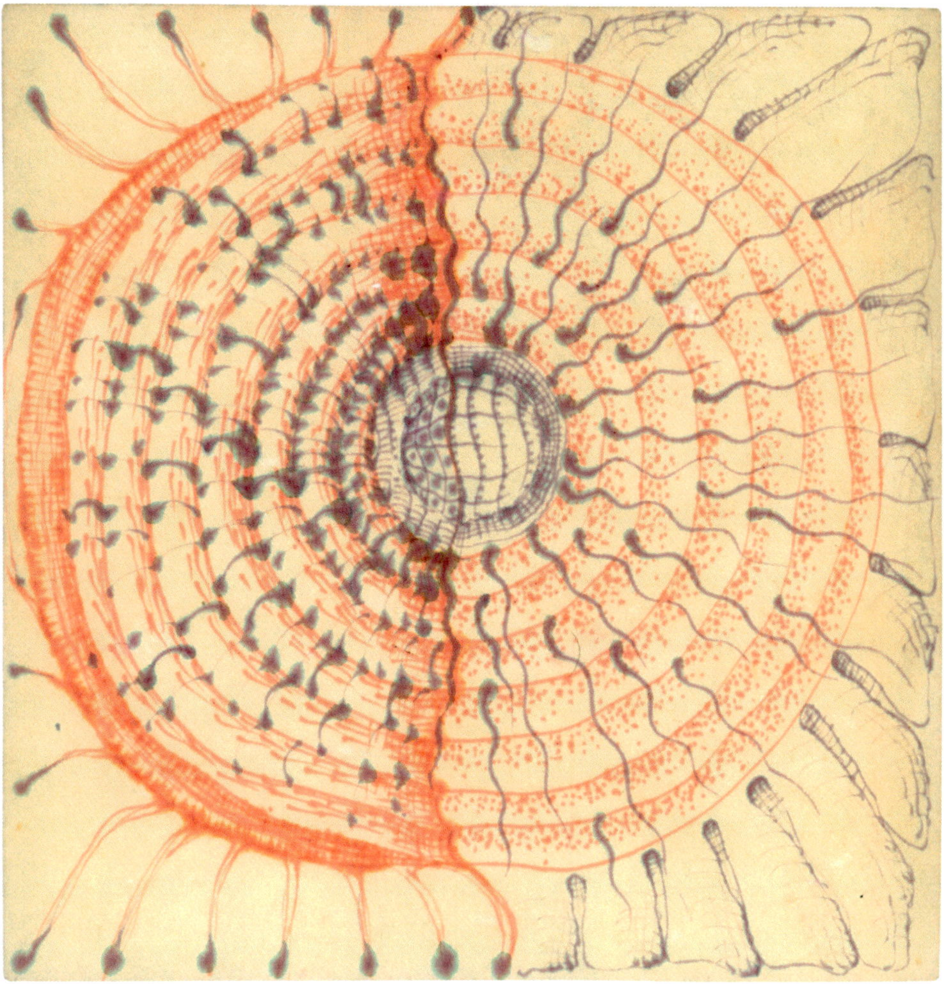

PL. 19 Jordan Belson, *Brain Drawing,* 1952

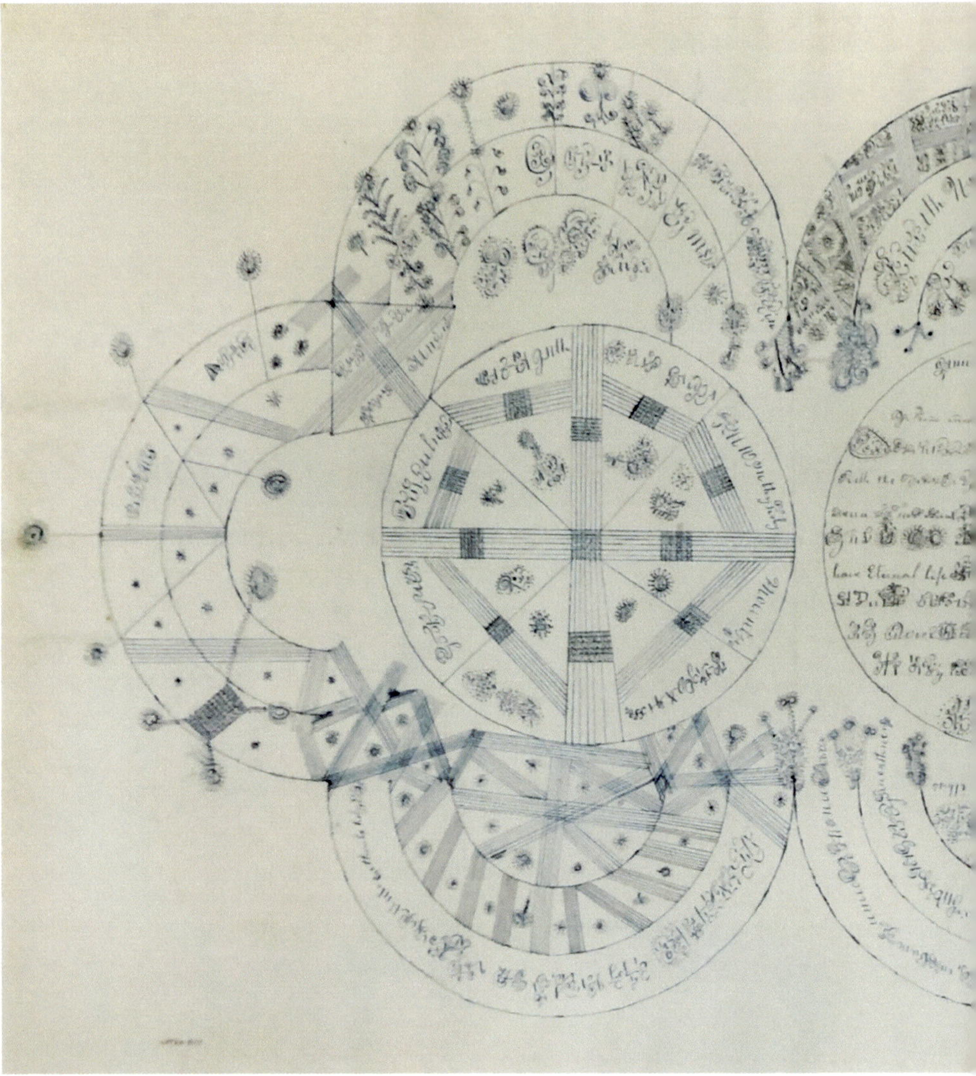

PL. 20 Unknown Shaker artist, *Word of the Saviour*, 1843

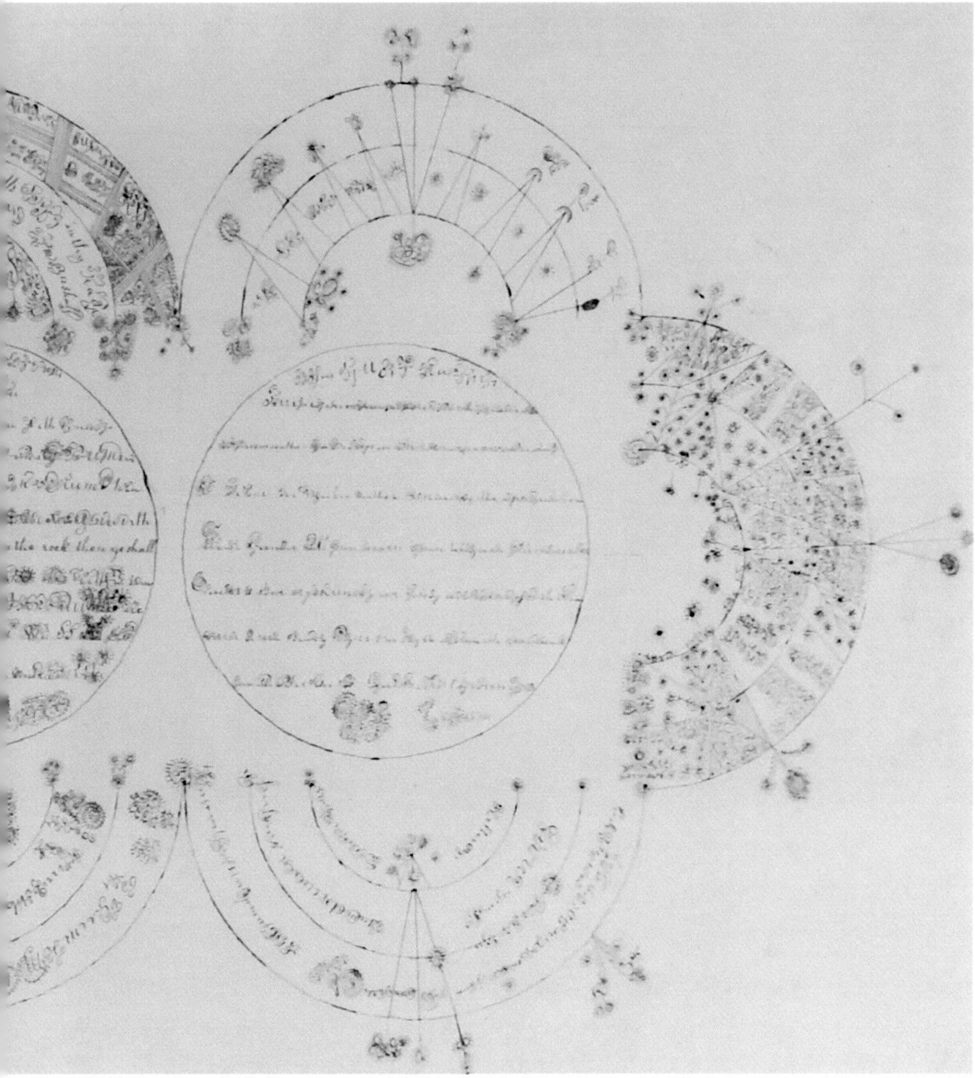

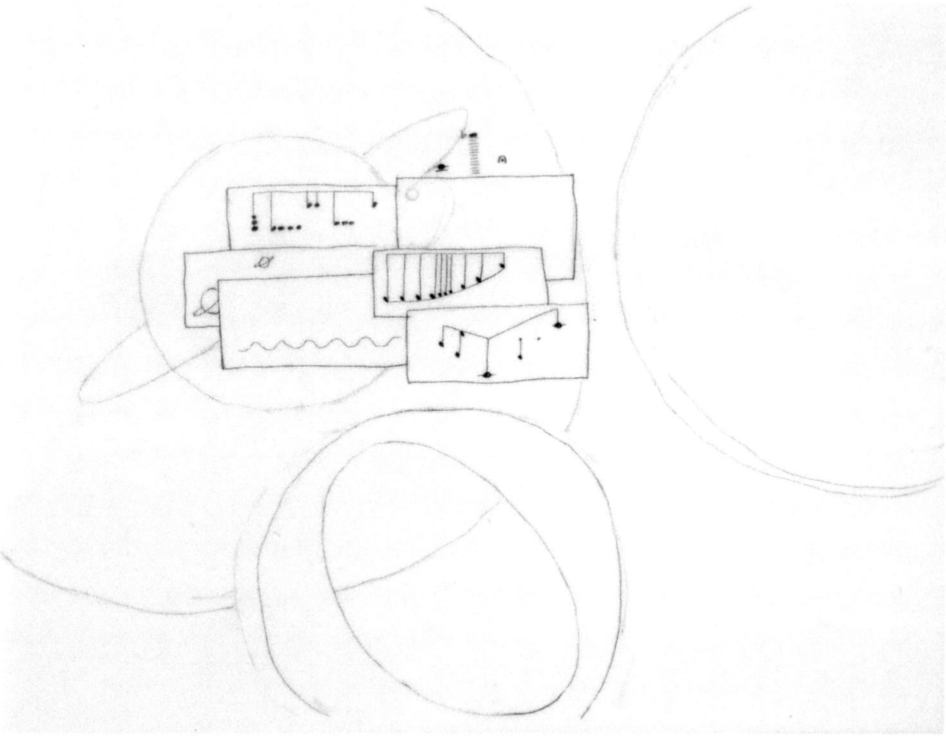

PL. 21 Bernadette Van-Huy, *Home Improvements*, 2019

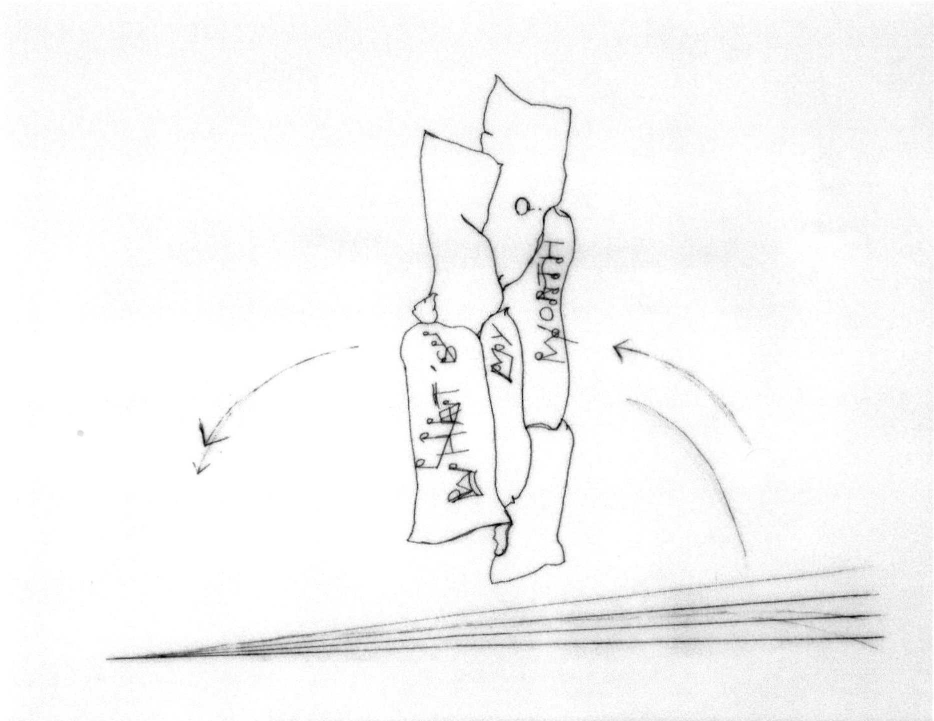

PL. 22 Bernadette Van-Huy, *Spinning with Spinoza*, 2019

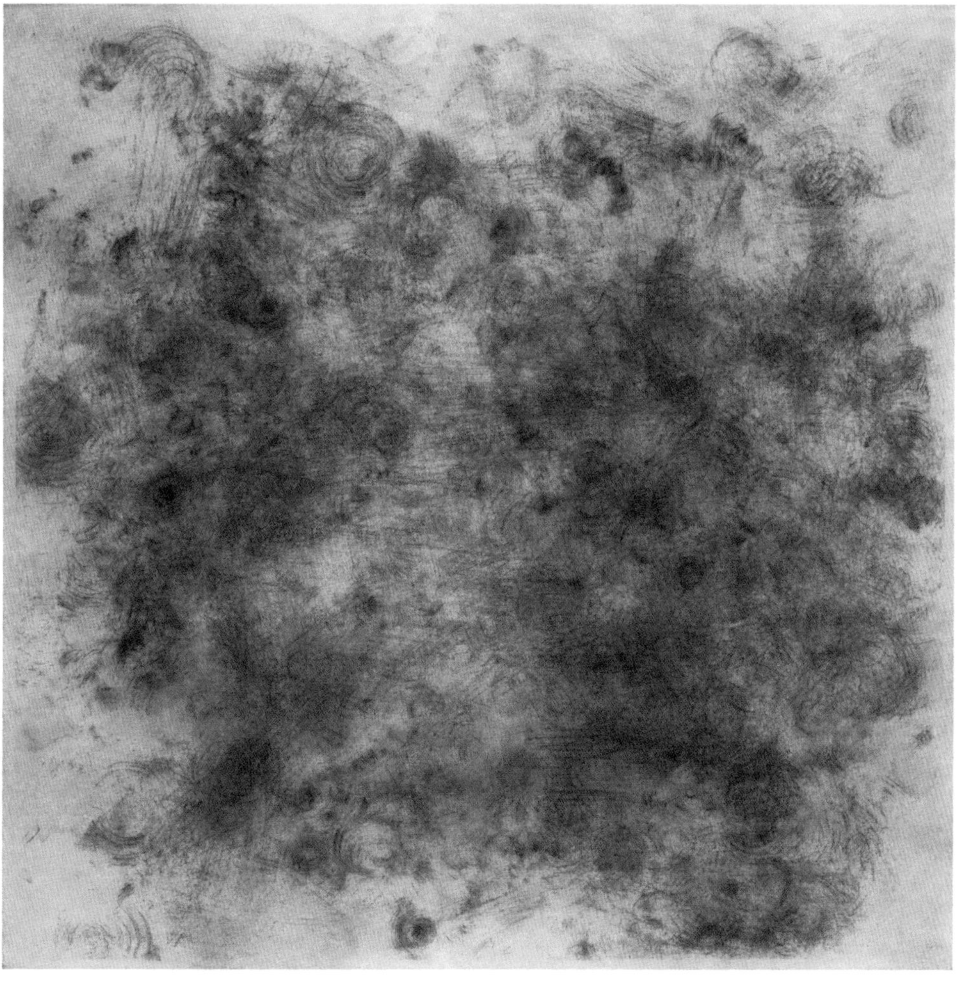

PL. 23 Julia Phillips, *Dance Marks*, 2014

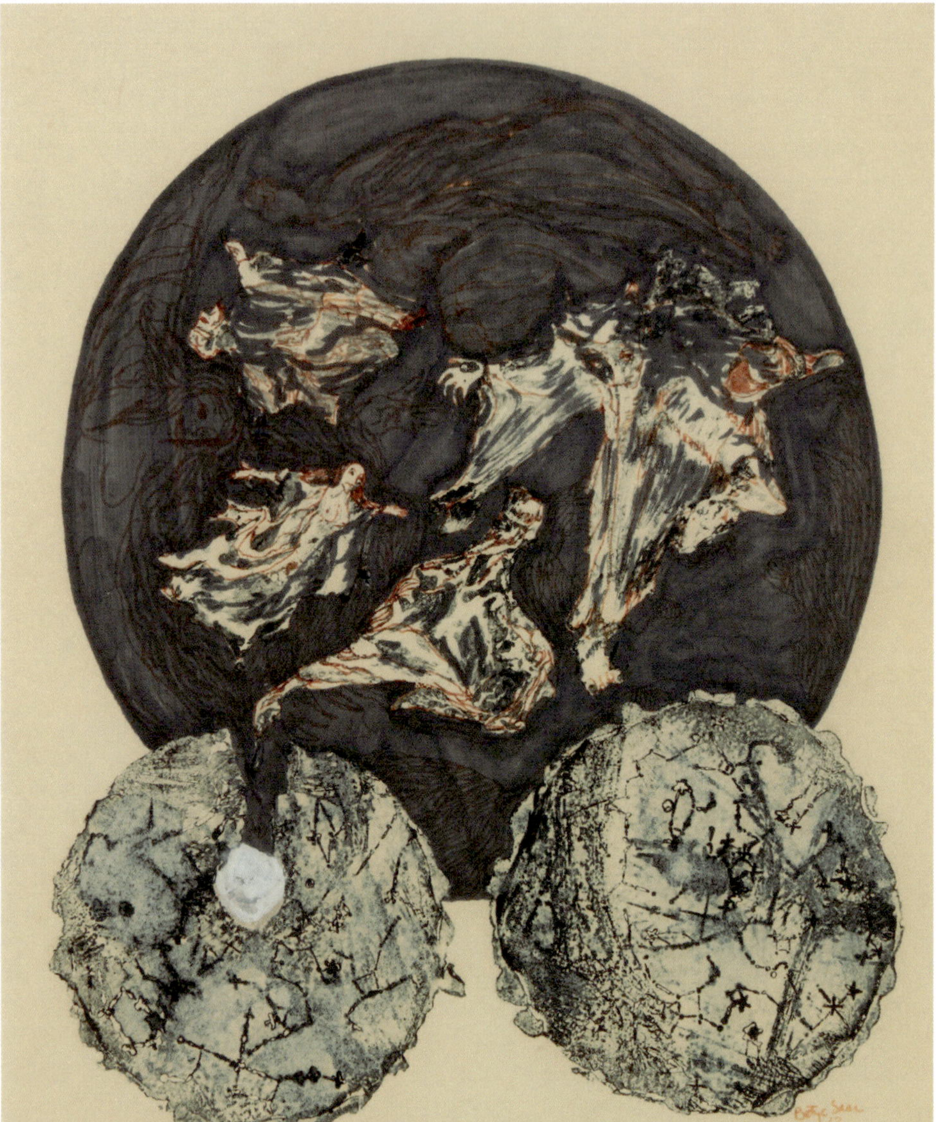

PL. 24 Betye Saar, *Taurus*, 1967

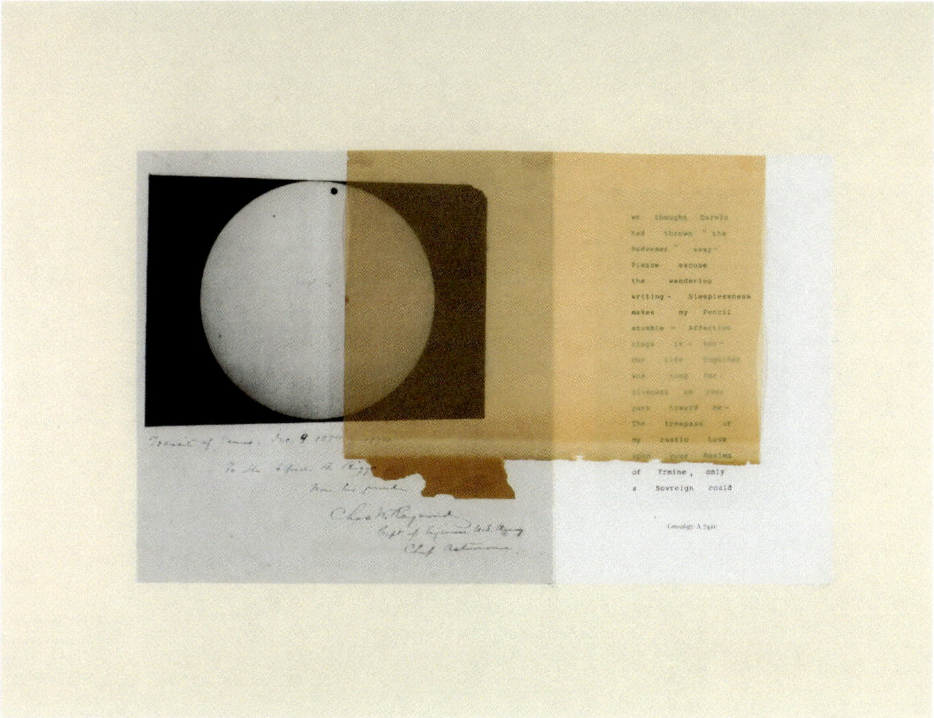

PL. 25 Janet Malcolm, *Ermine* (from the *Emily Dickinson Series*), 2013

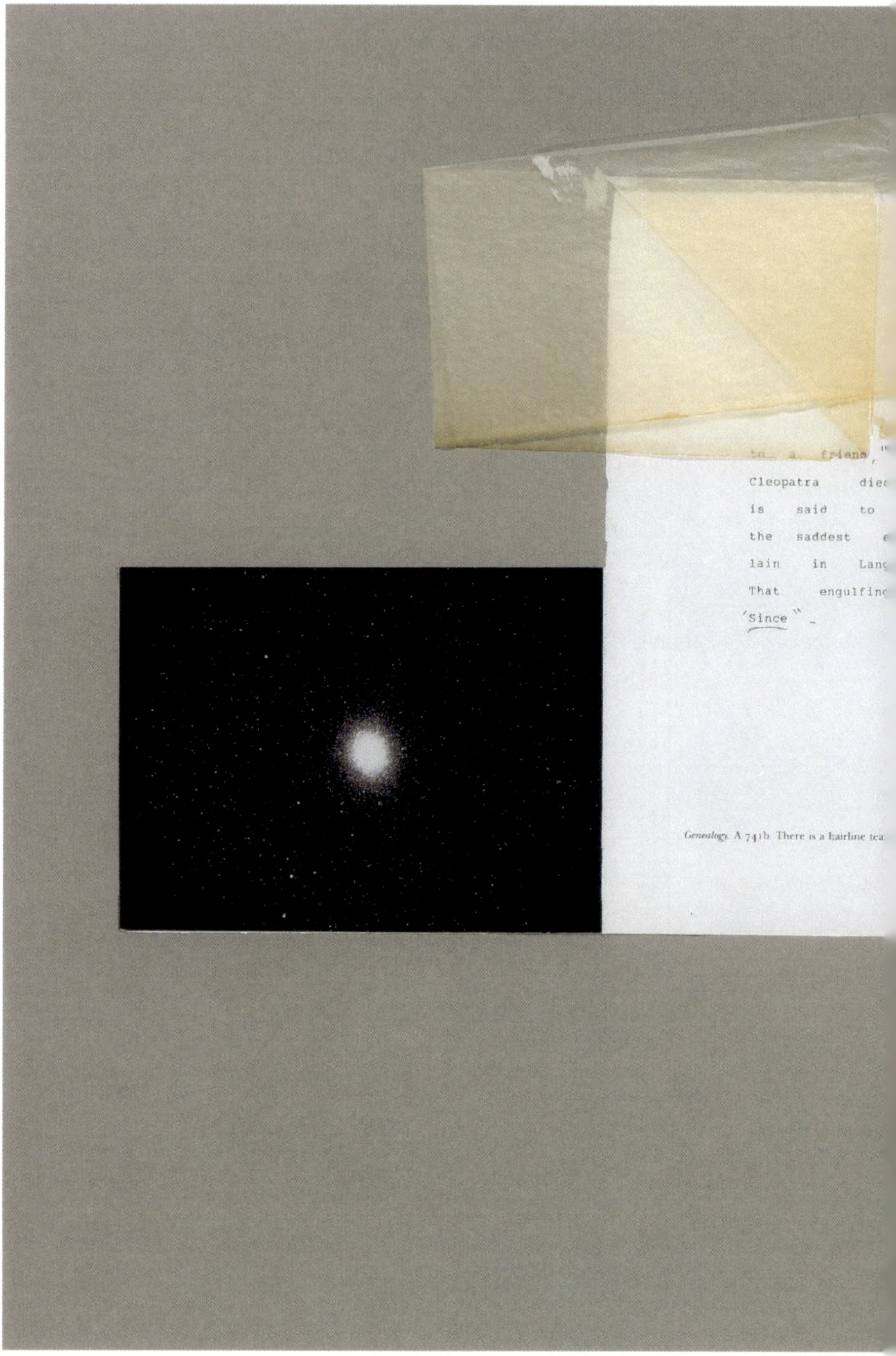

PL. 26 Janet Malcolm, *Cleopatra* (from the *Emily Dickinson Series*), 2013

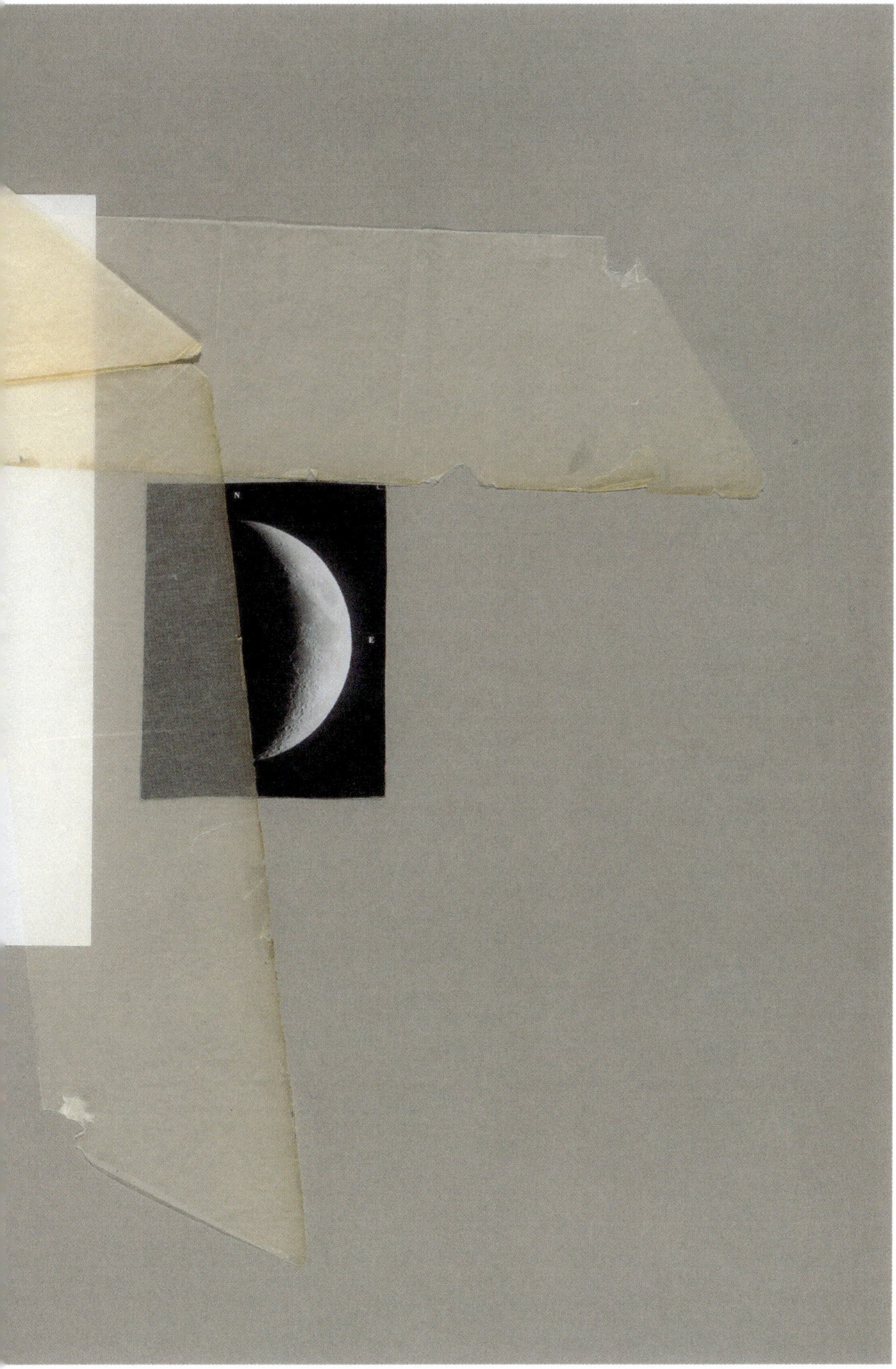
N
E

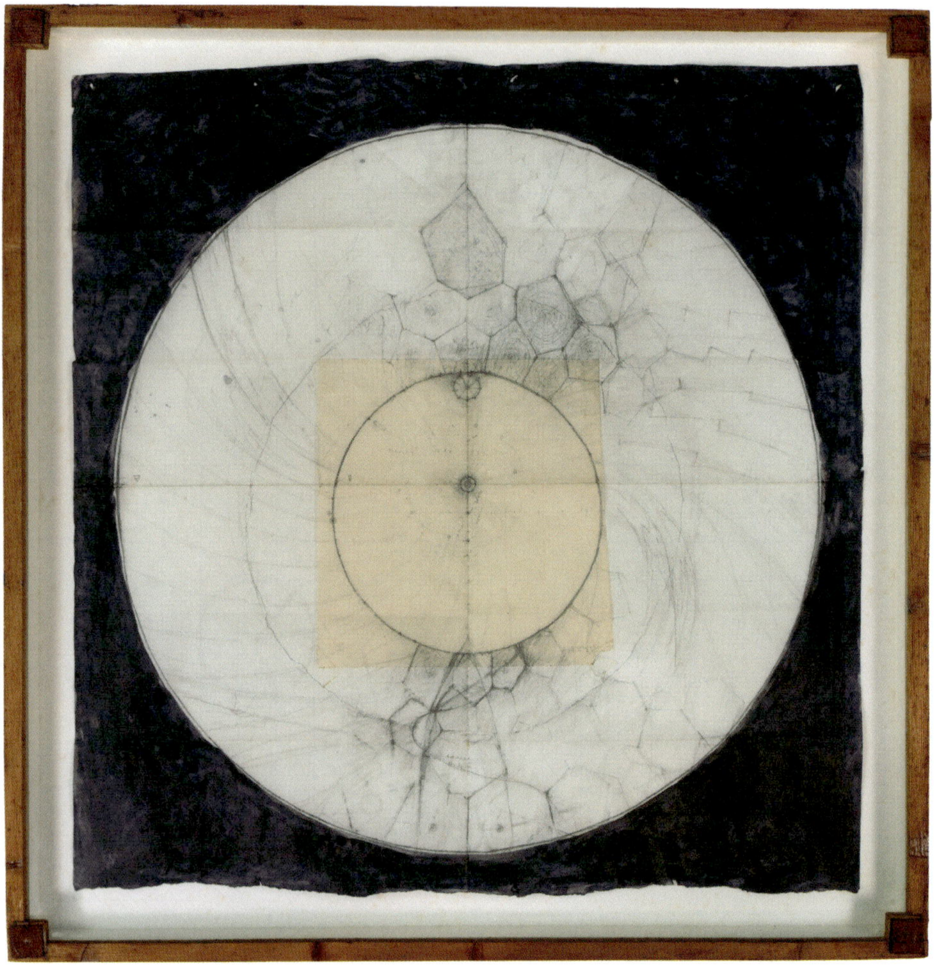

PL. 27 Mel Chin, *Study for Mercury: The Principle of Polarity–The Orbital Rebus*, 1987

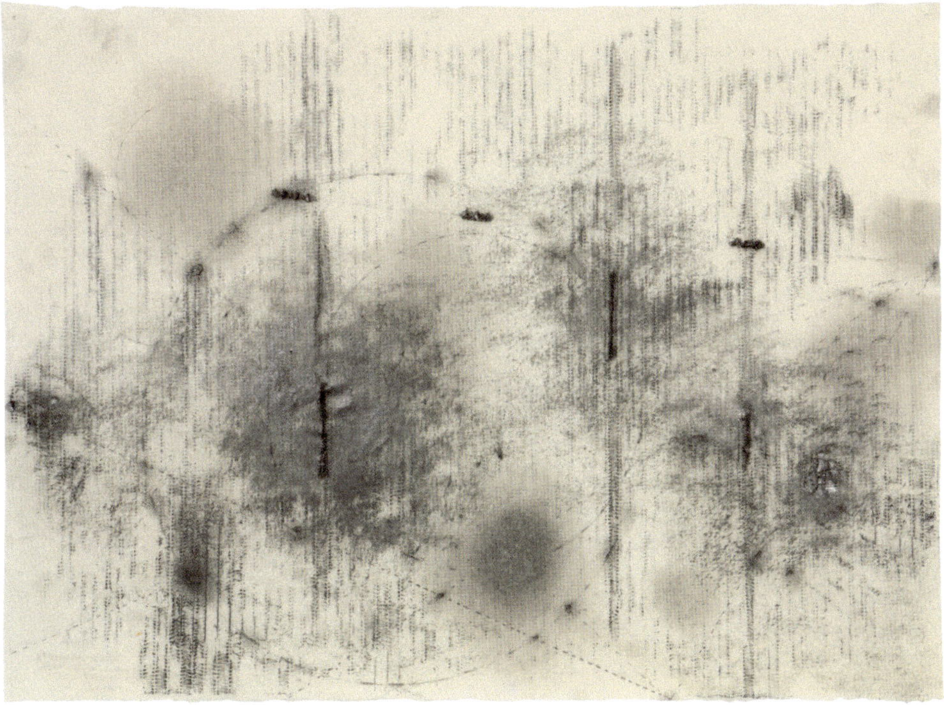

PL. 28 Jack Whitten, *Radiator Drawing #5*, 2010

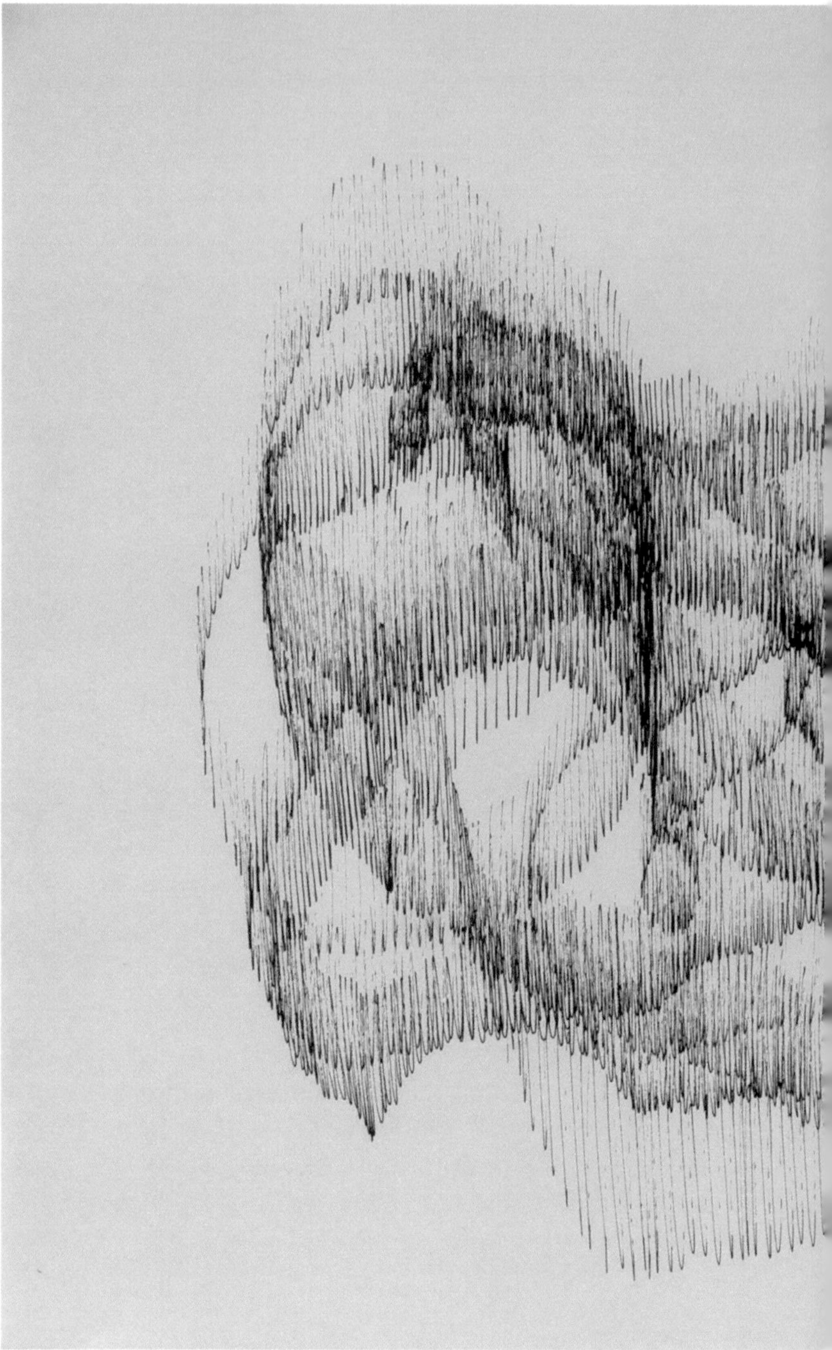

PL. 29 Cameron, *Pluto Transiting the Twelfth House*, 1978-86

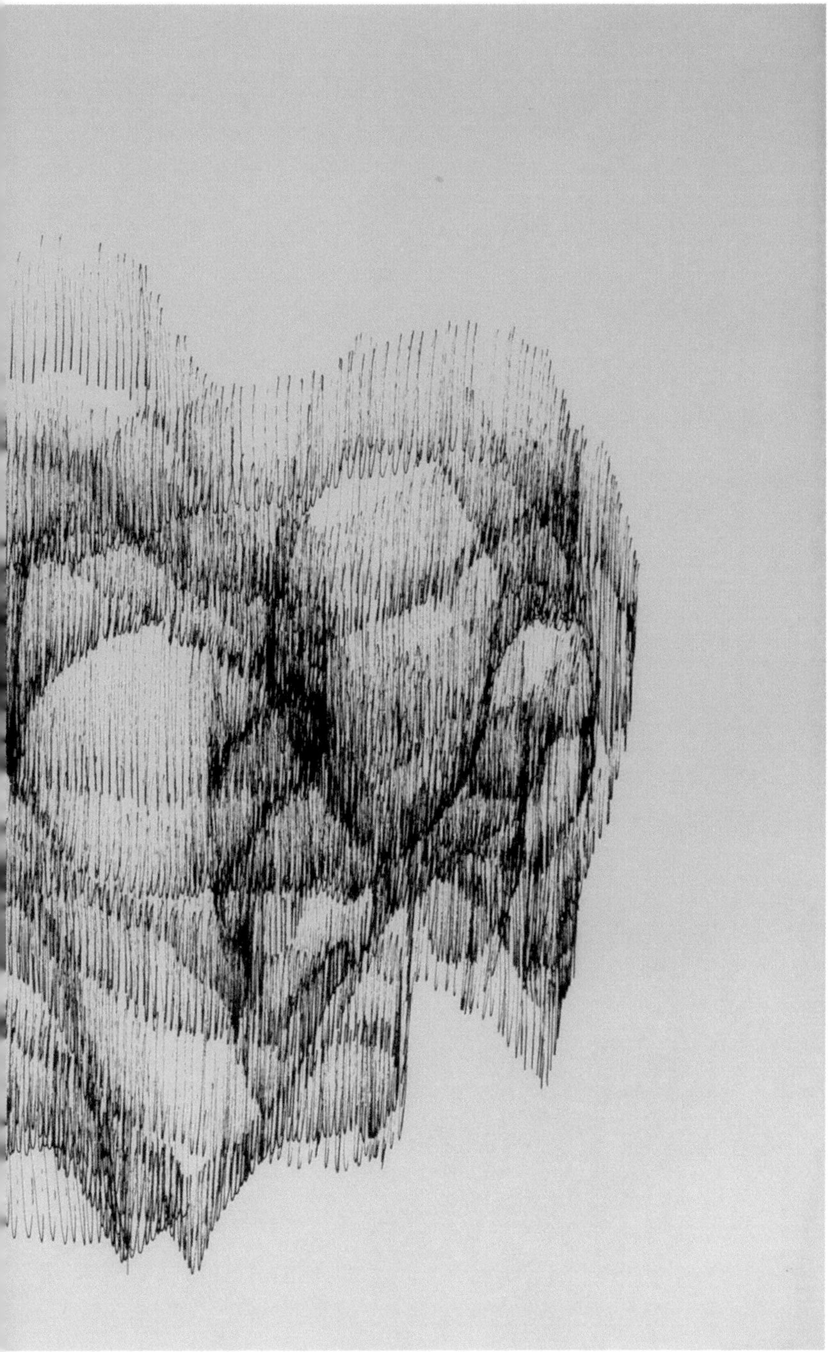

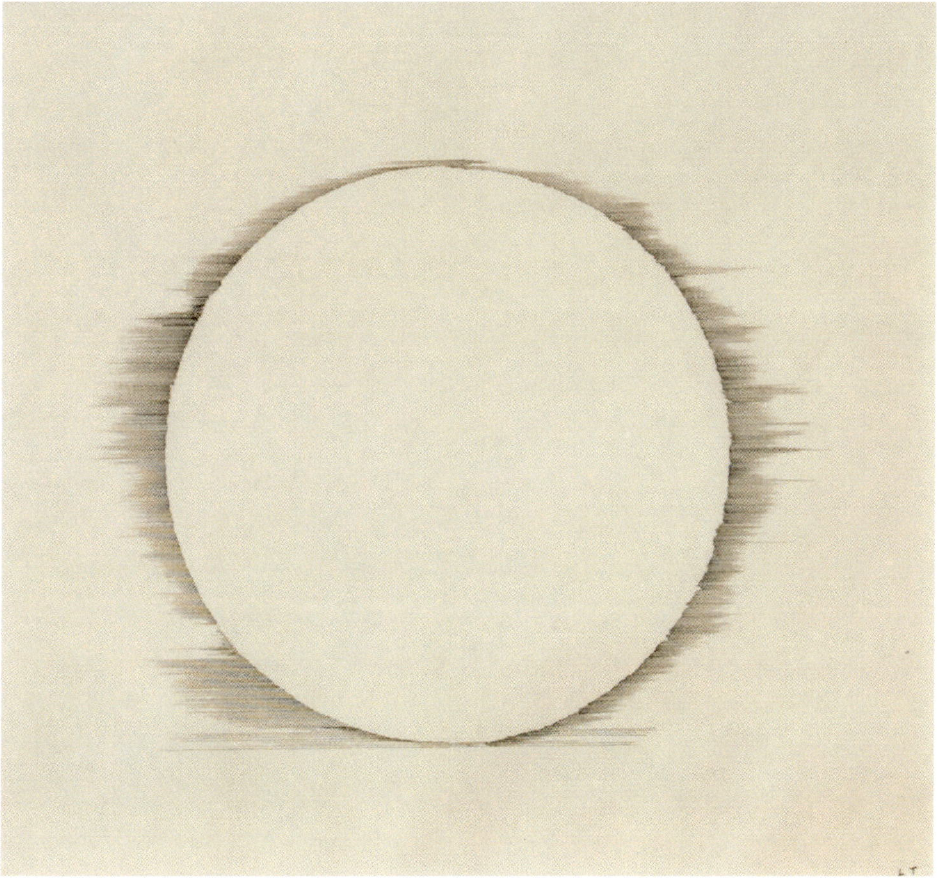

PL. 30 Lenore Tawney, *Eclipse*, 1965

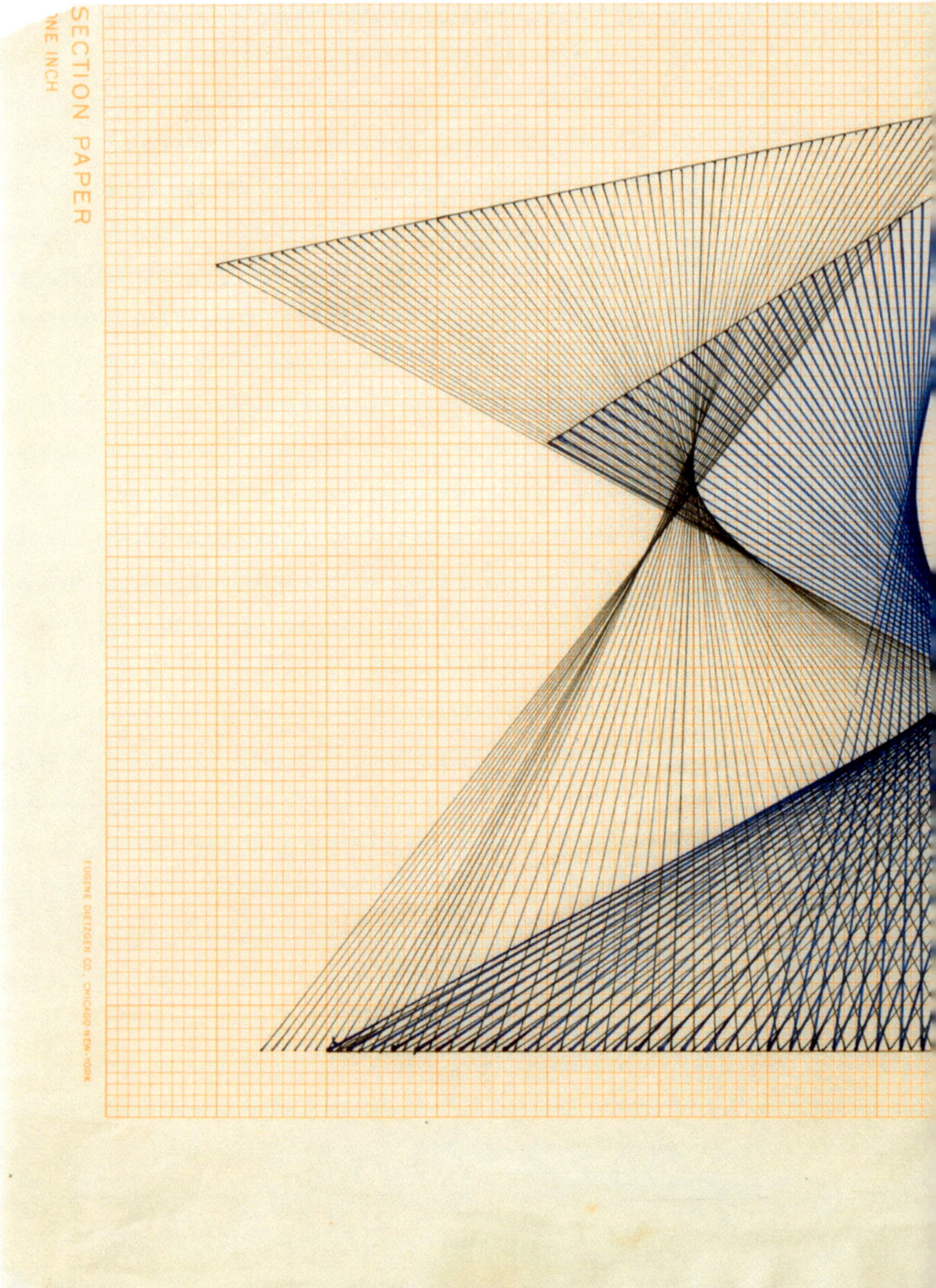

PL. 31 Lenore Tawney, *Untitled*, 1965

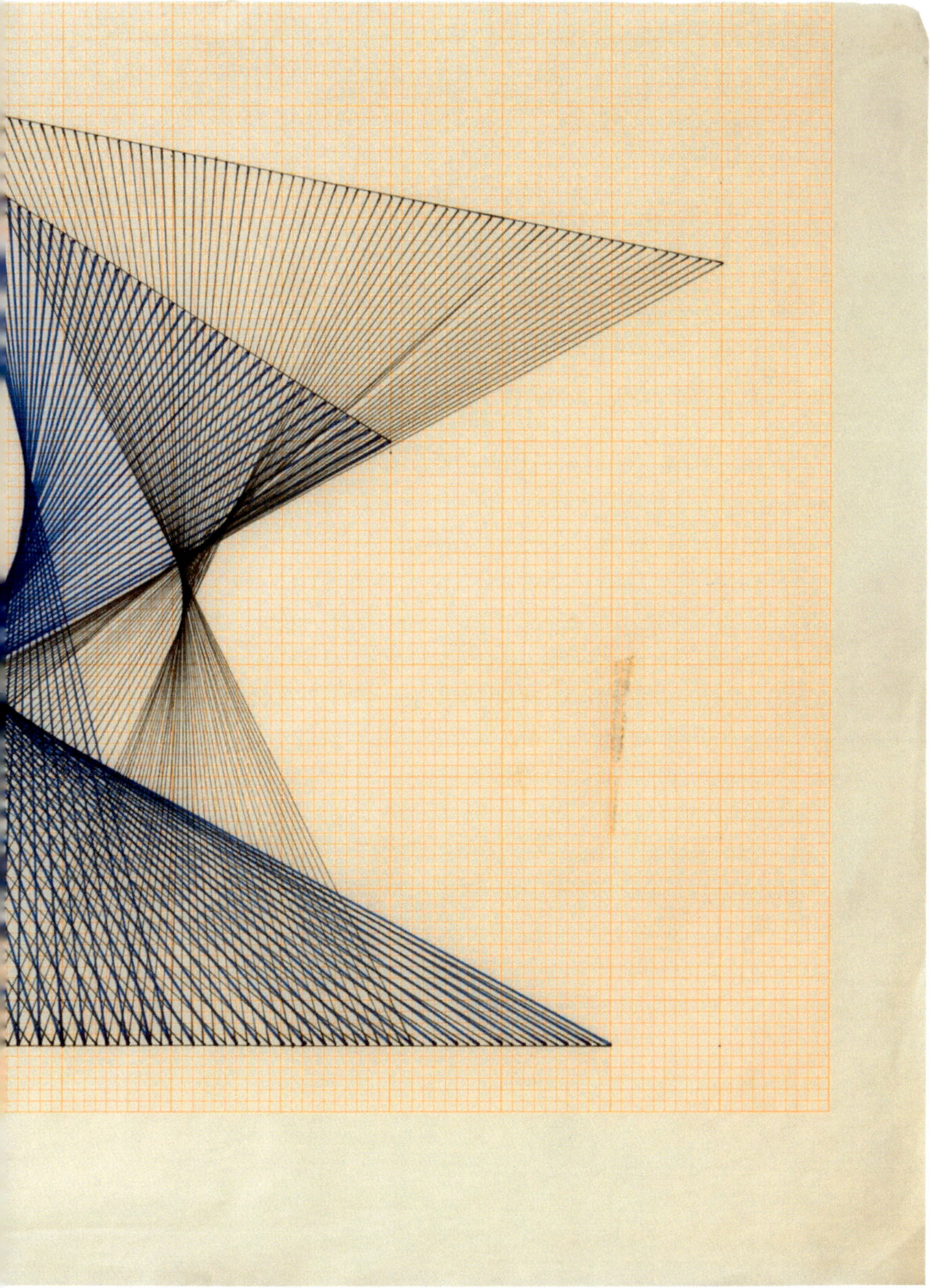

PL. 32 Yutaka Matsuzawa, *Untitled*, 1960–63

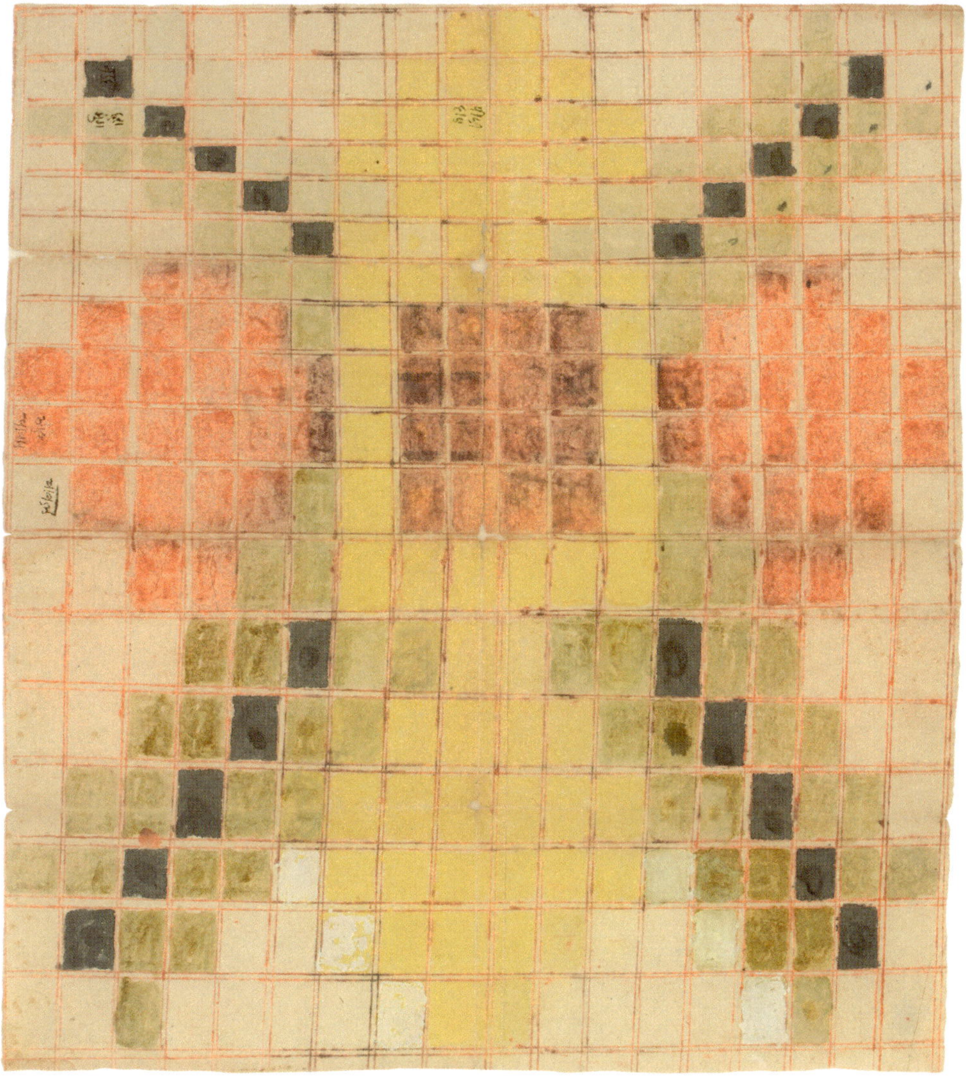

PL. 33 Unknown artist, Rajasthan, *Sarvatobhadra Yantra*, c. 18th–19th century

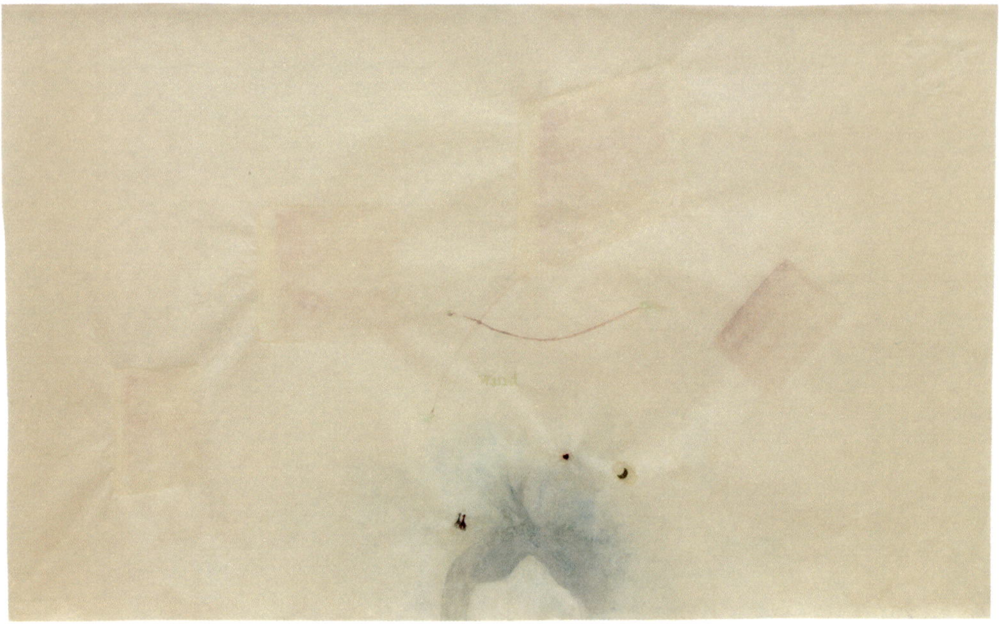

PL. 34 Cici Wu, *The Disappearance of Yu Man-hon (storyboard 02)*, 2017

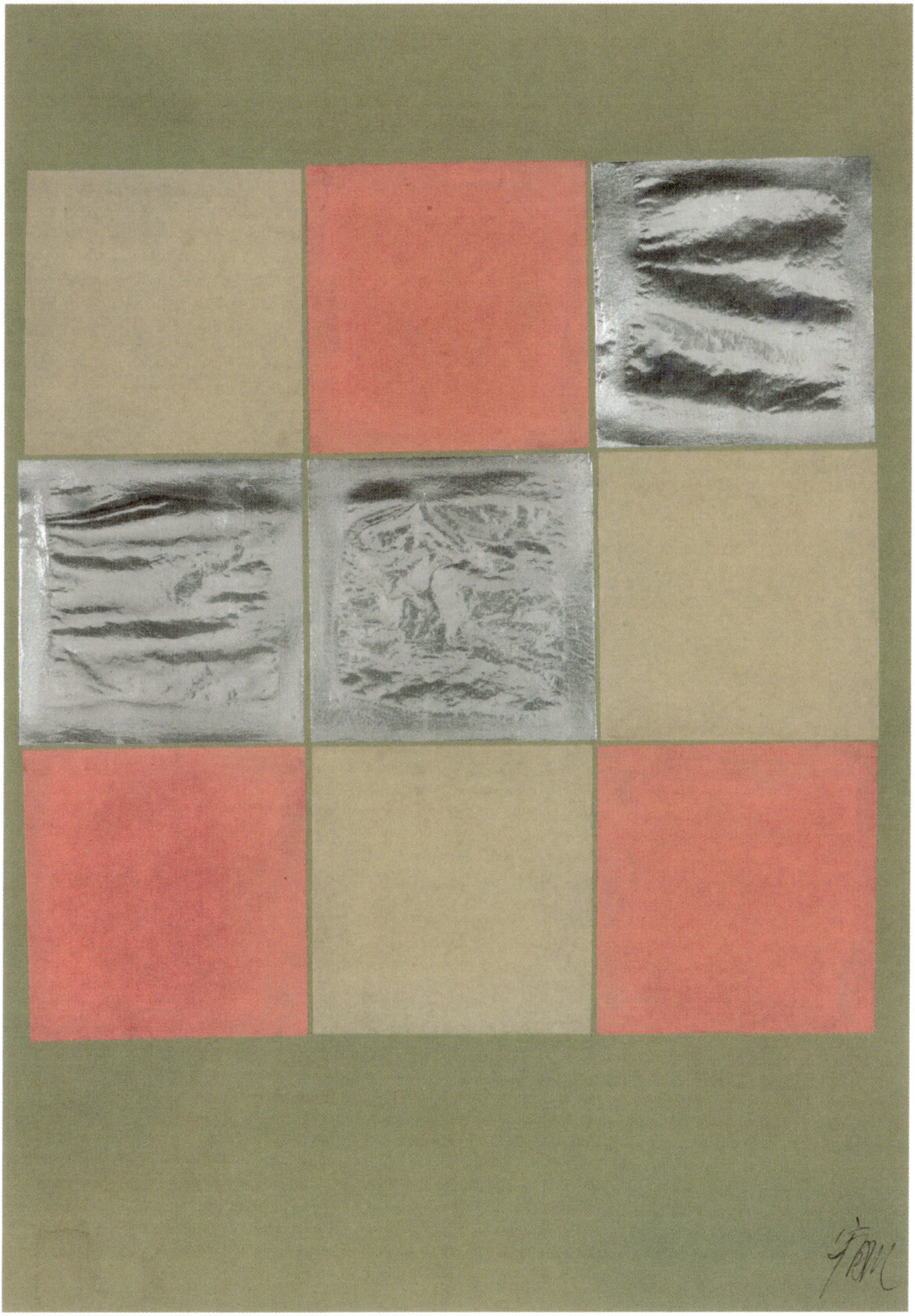

PL. 35 Yutaka Matsuzawa, *Untitled*, 1960-63

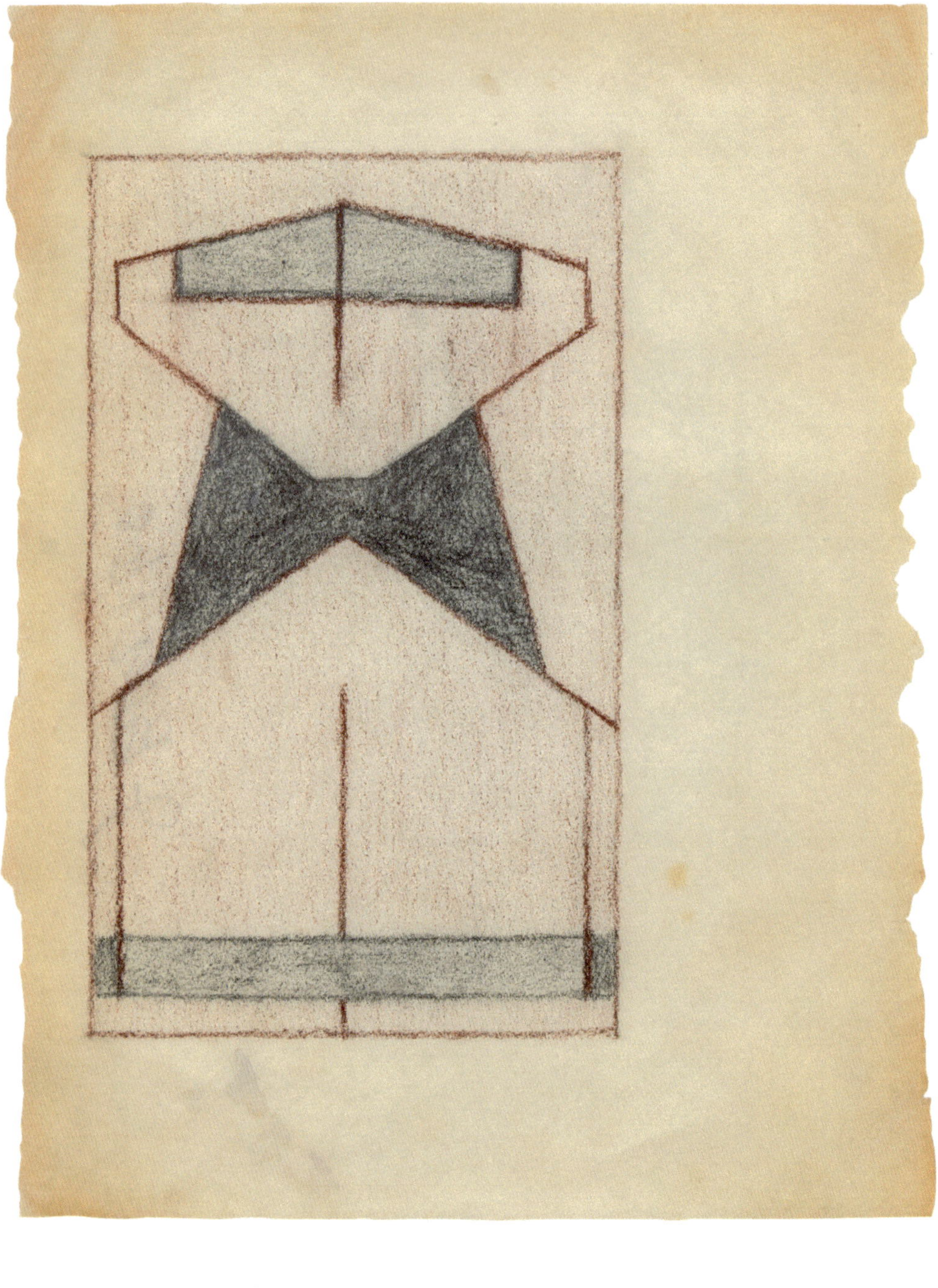

PL. 36 Jo Baer, *Untitled*, 1960

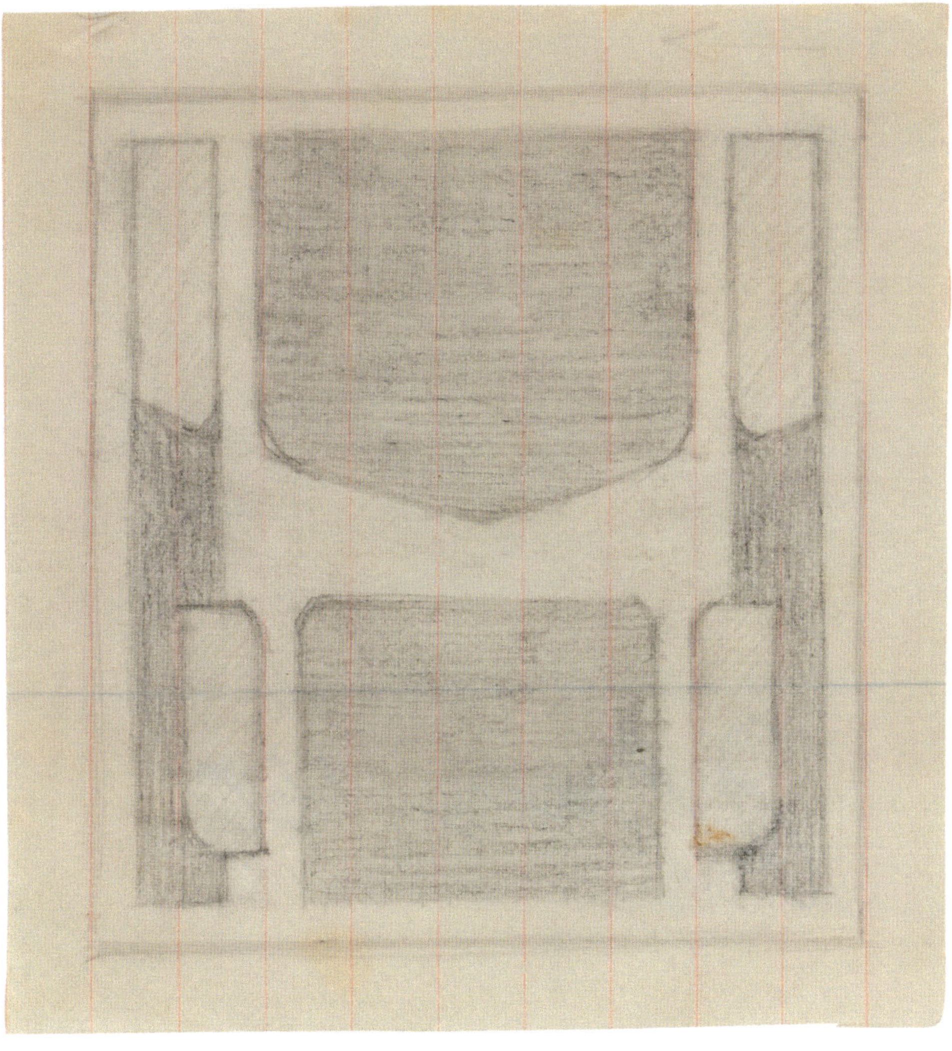

PL. 37 Jo Baer, *Untitled*, 1960

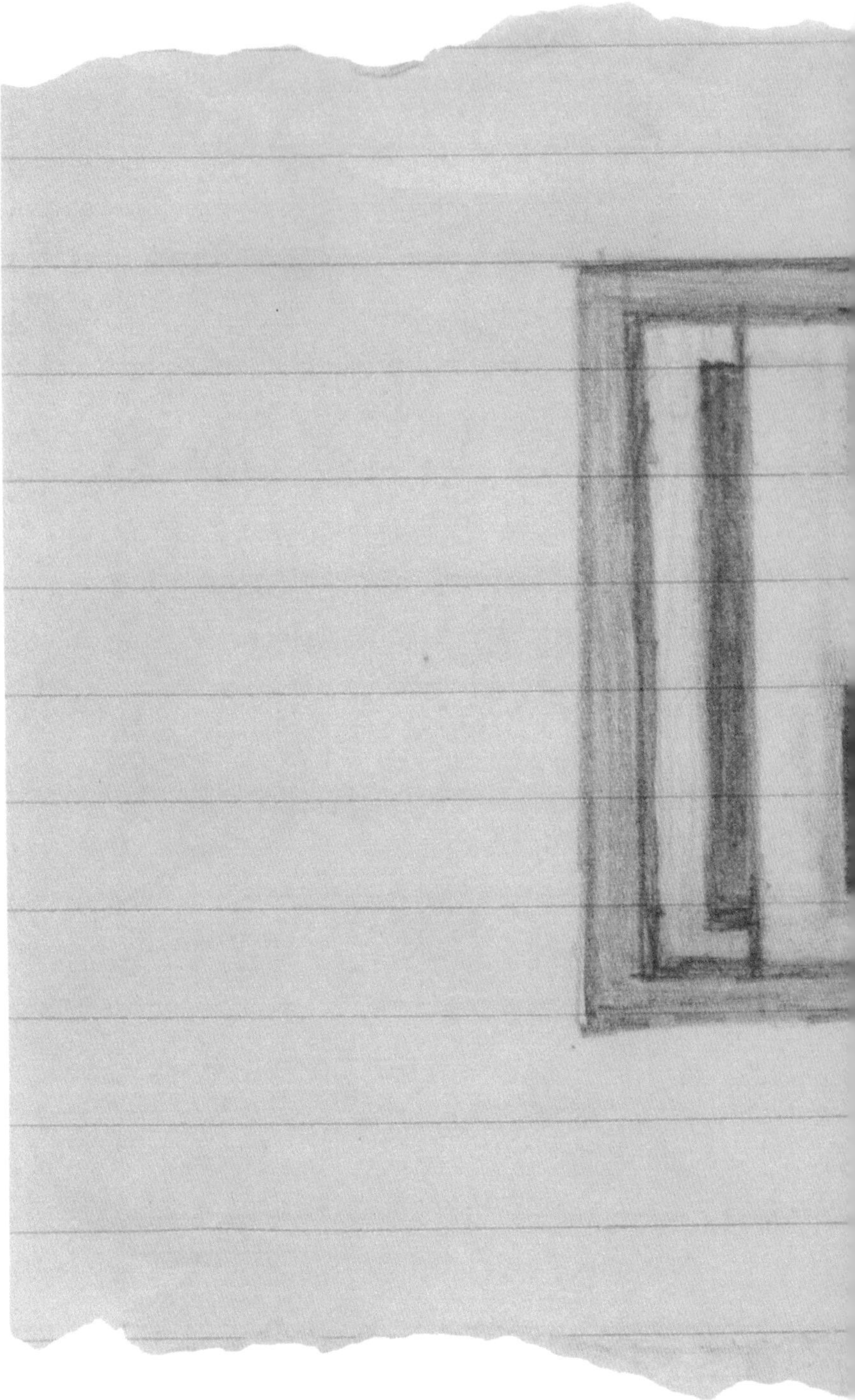

PL. 38 Jo Baer, *Untitled*, 1960

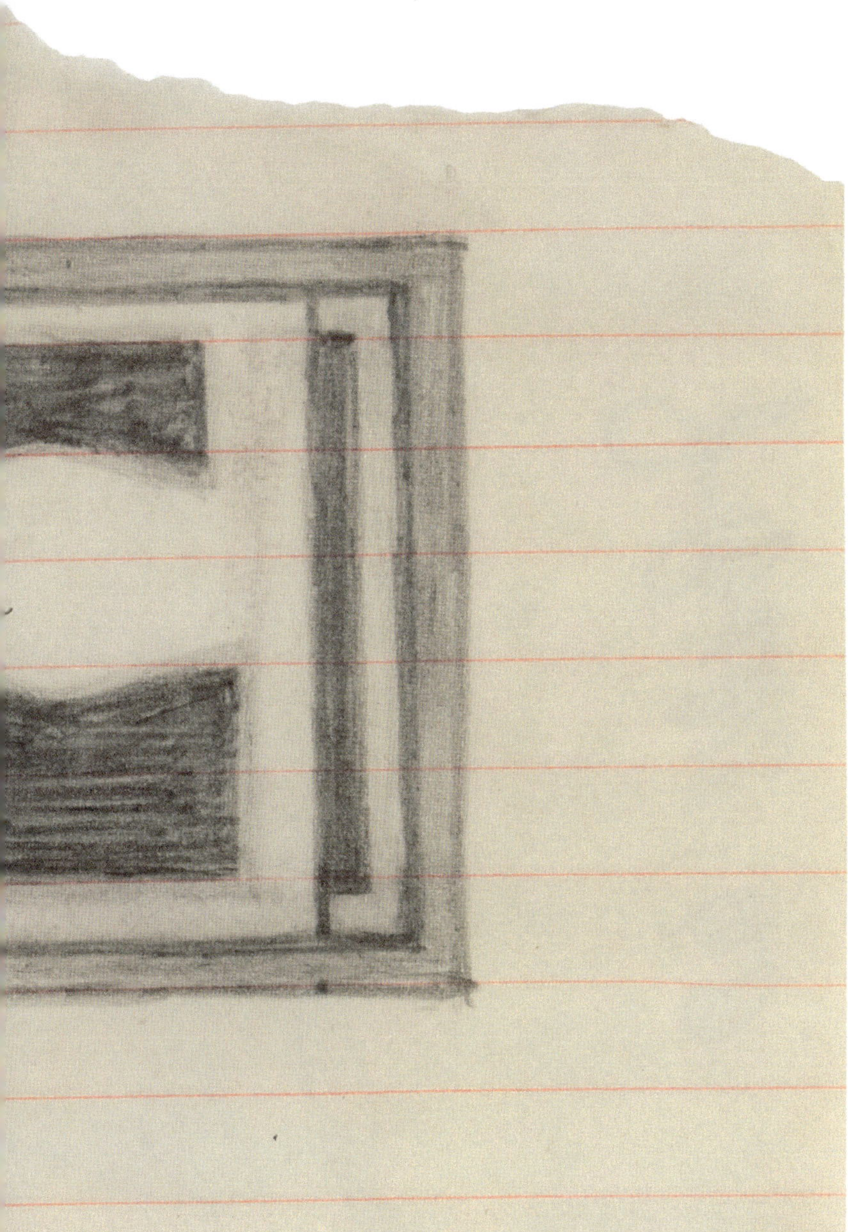

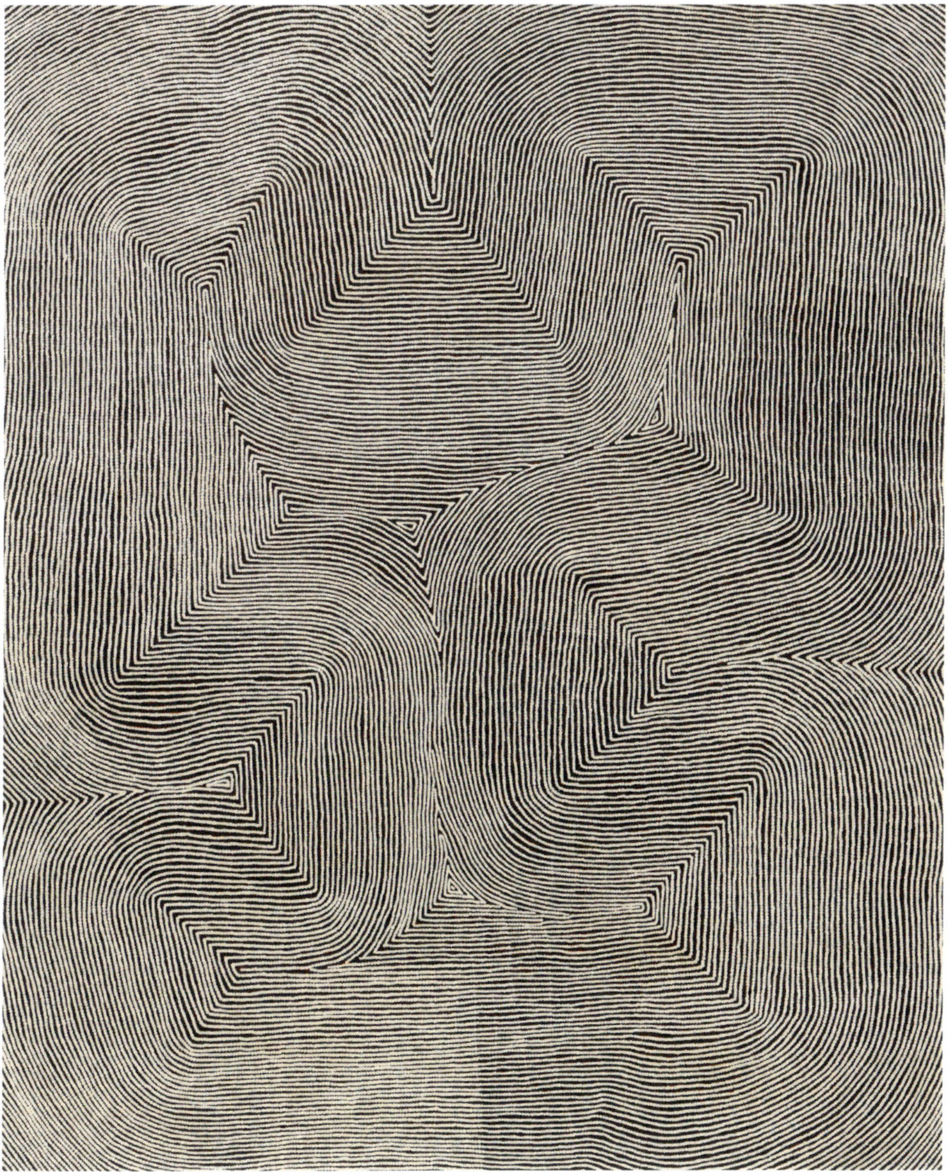

PL. 39 Warlimpirrnga Tjapaltjarri, *Maruwa*, 2017

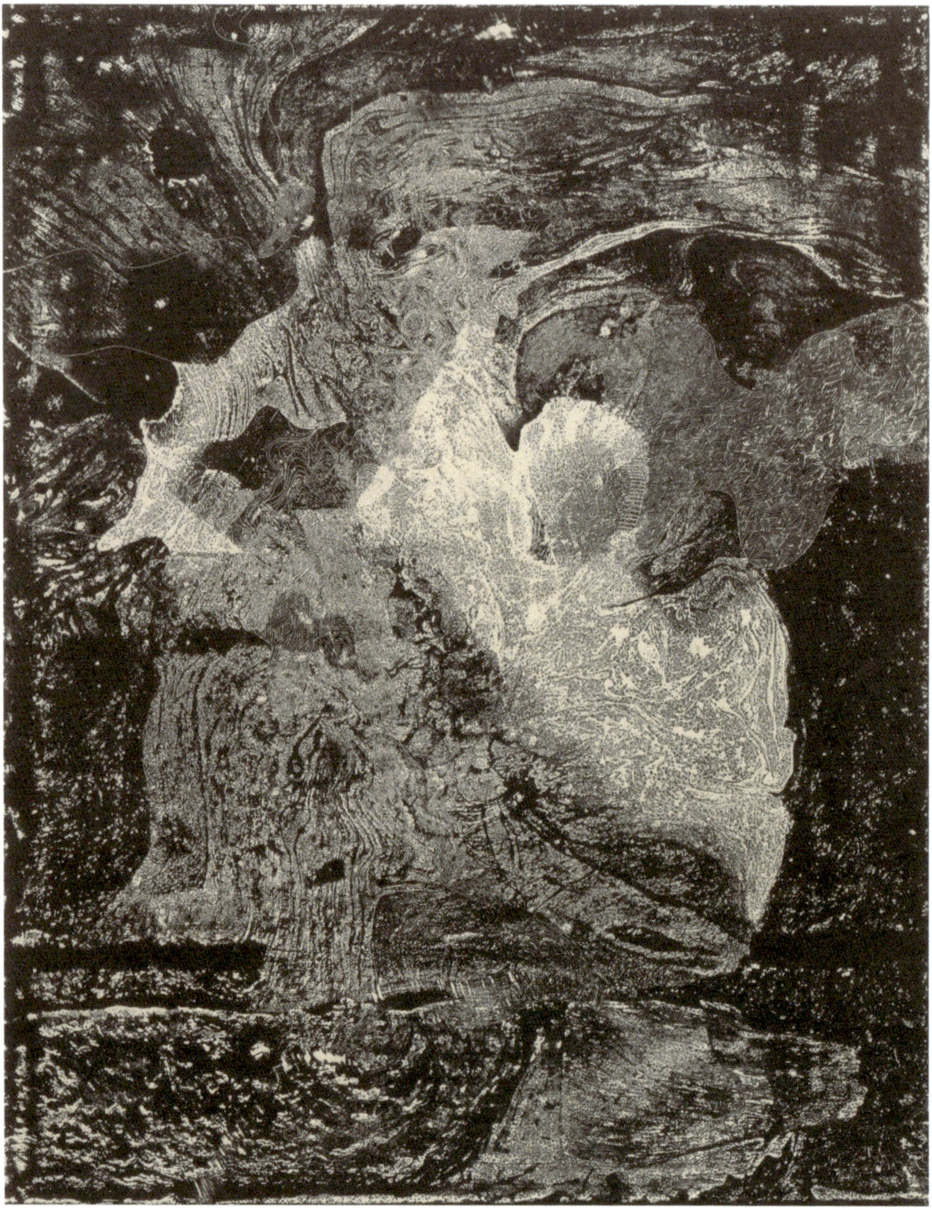

PL. 40 Mohammed O. Khalil, *Bomb Cantata*, 1968

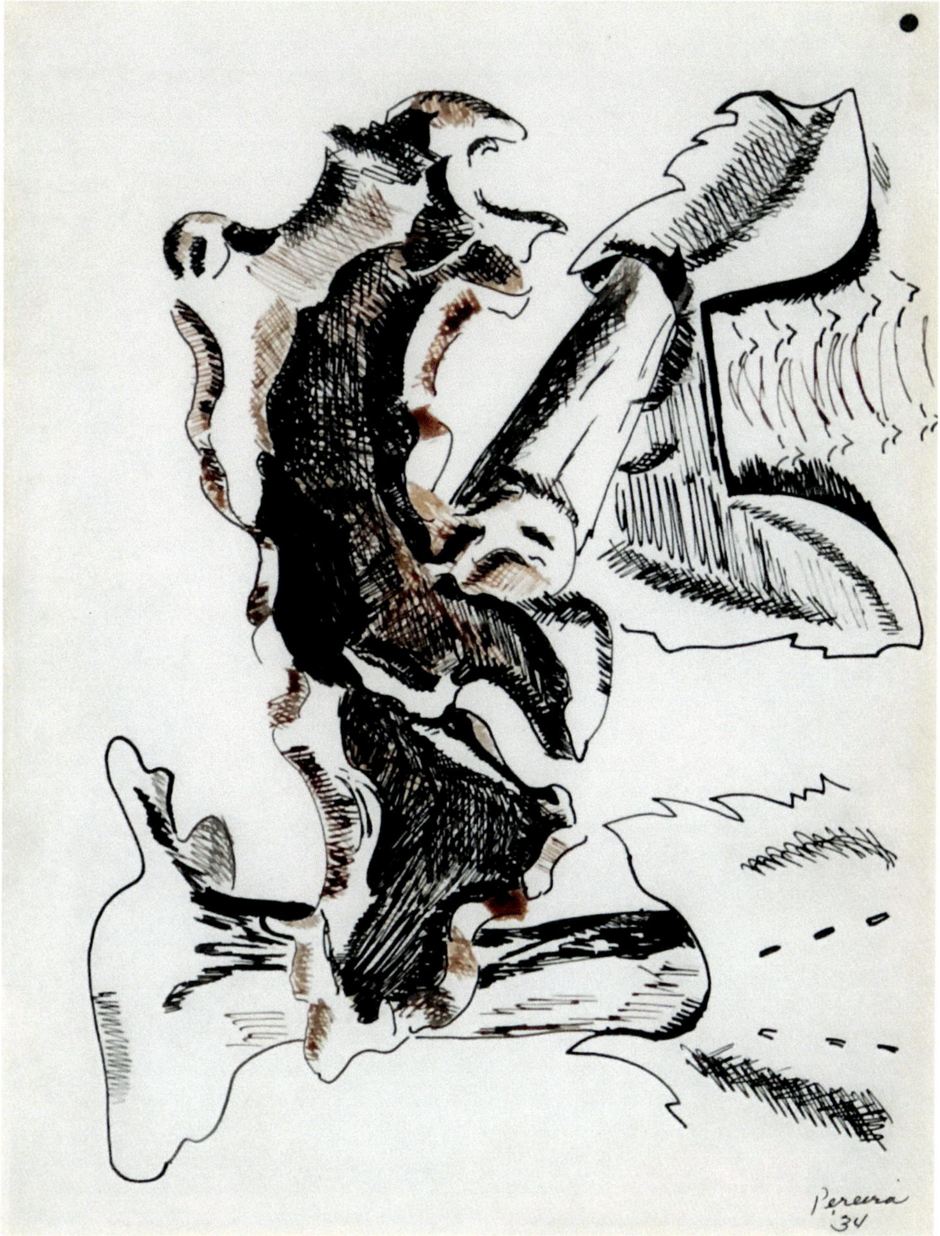

PL. 41 I. Rice Pereira, *Untitled*, 1934

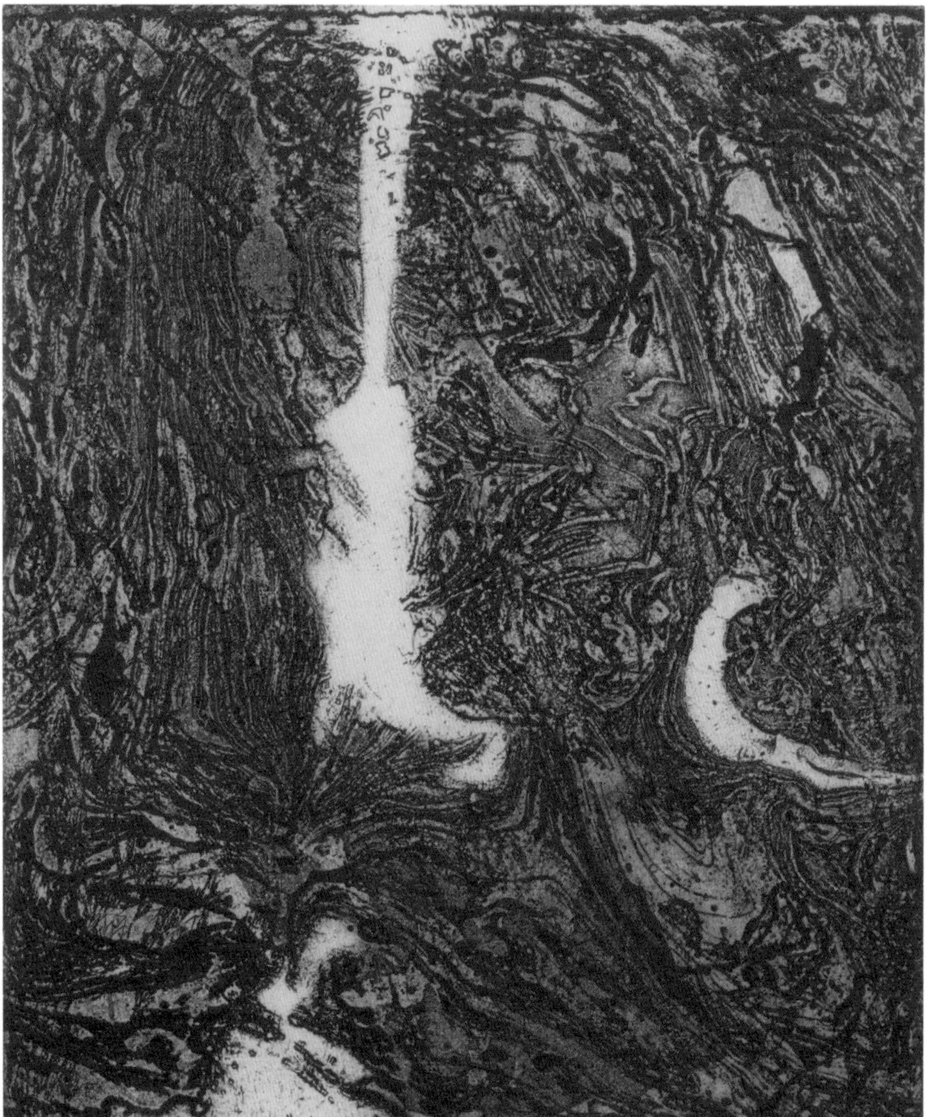

PL. 42 Mohammed O. Khalil, *The Second Queen*, 1974

PL. 43 Arnold J. Kemp, *Index*, 2021

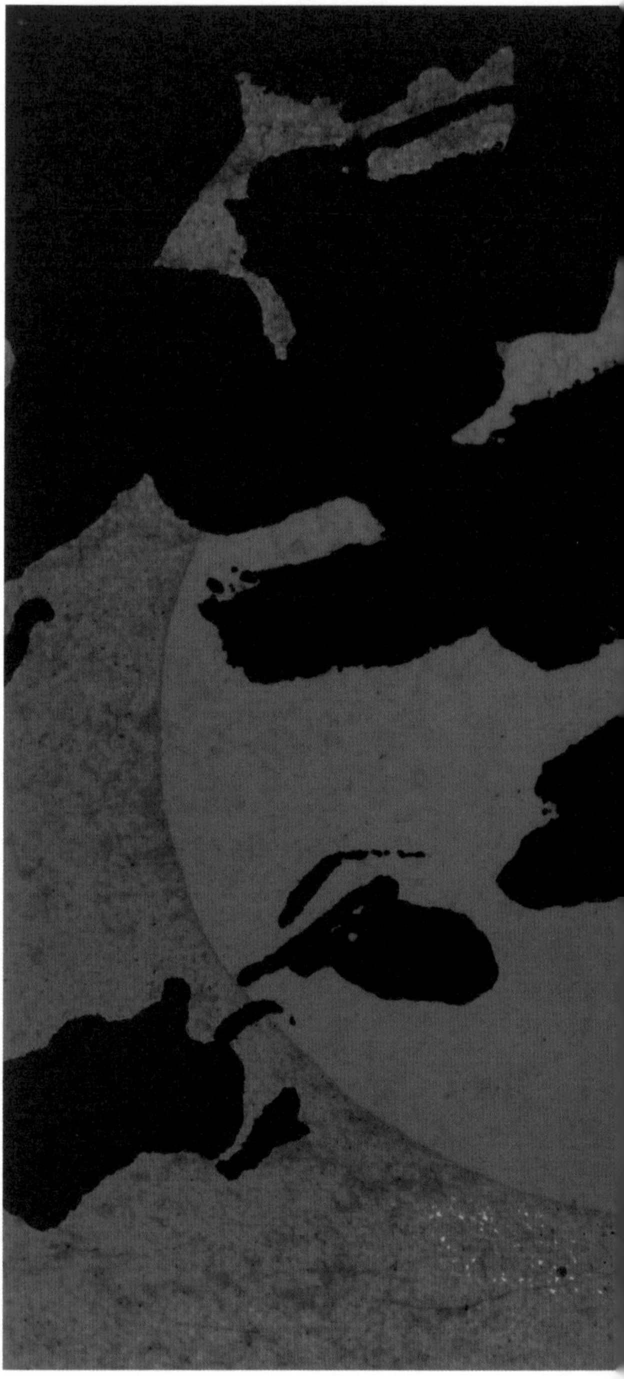

PL. 44 Steffani Jemison, *Black Utopia (Sol)*, 2017

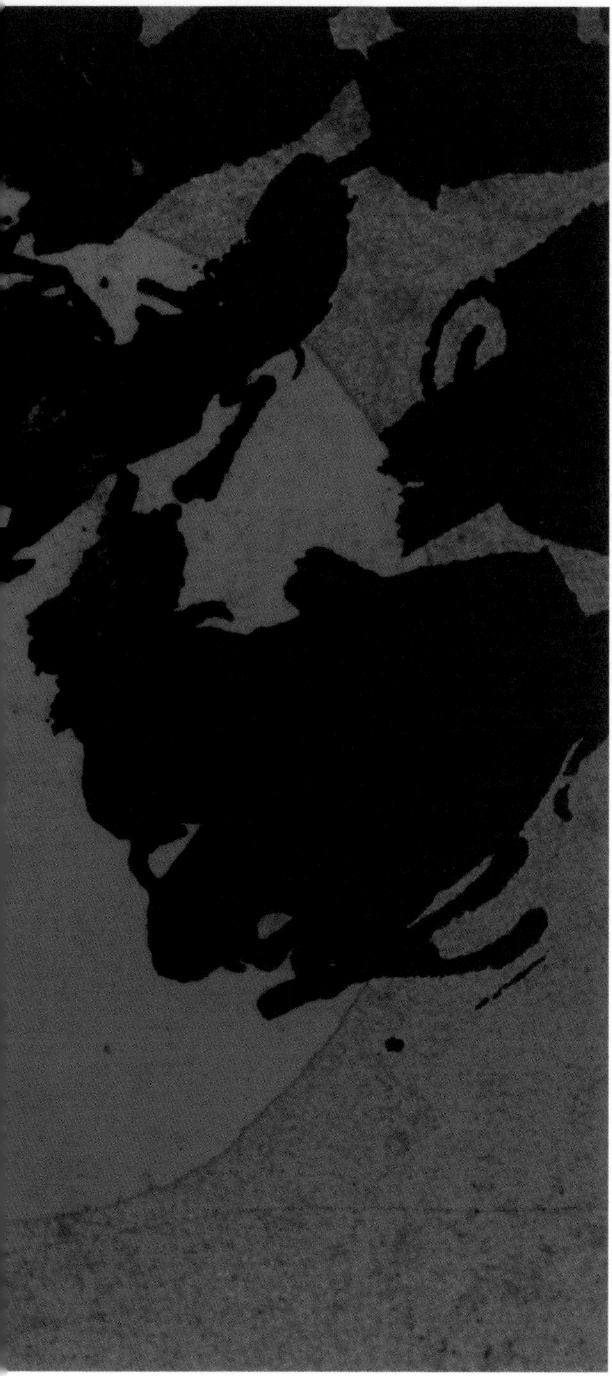

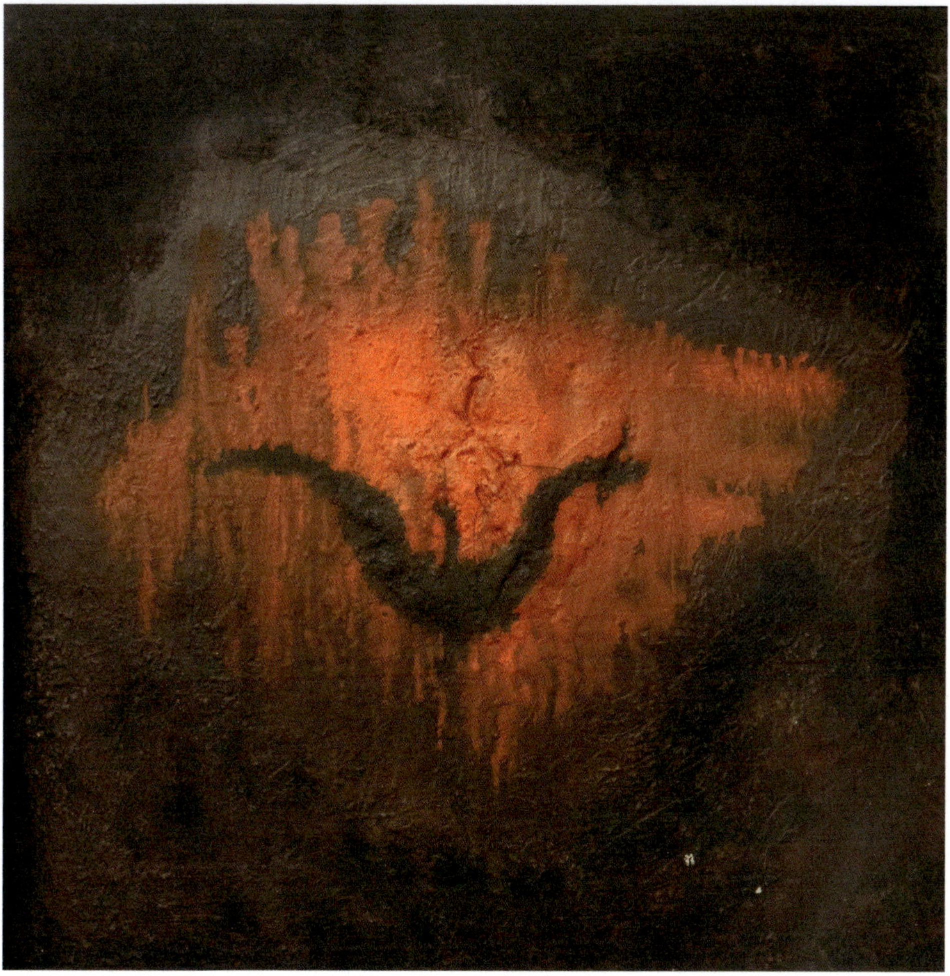

PL. 45 Yutaka Matsuzawa, *Untitled*, 1960–63

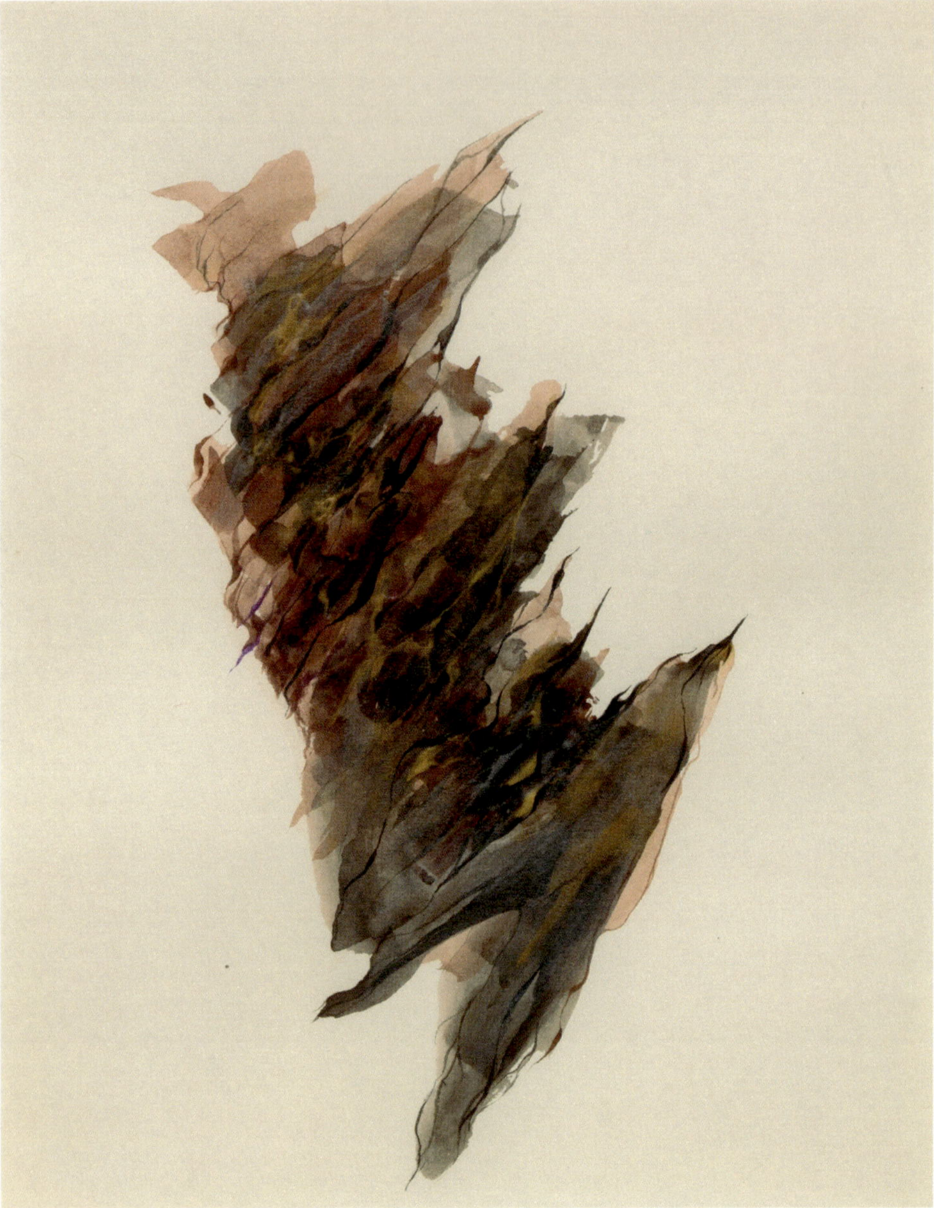

PL. 46 Cameron, *Untitled* (from the *Lion Path* series), n.d.

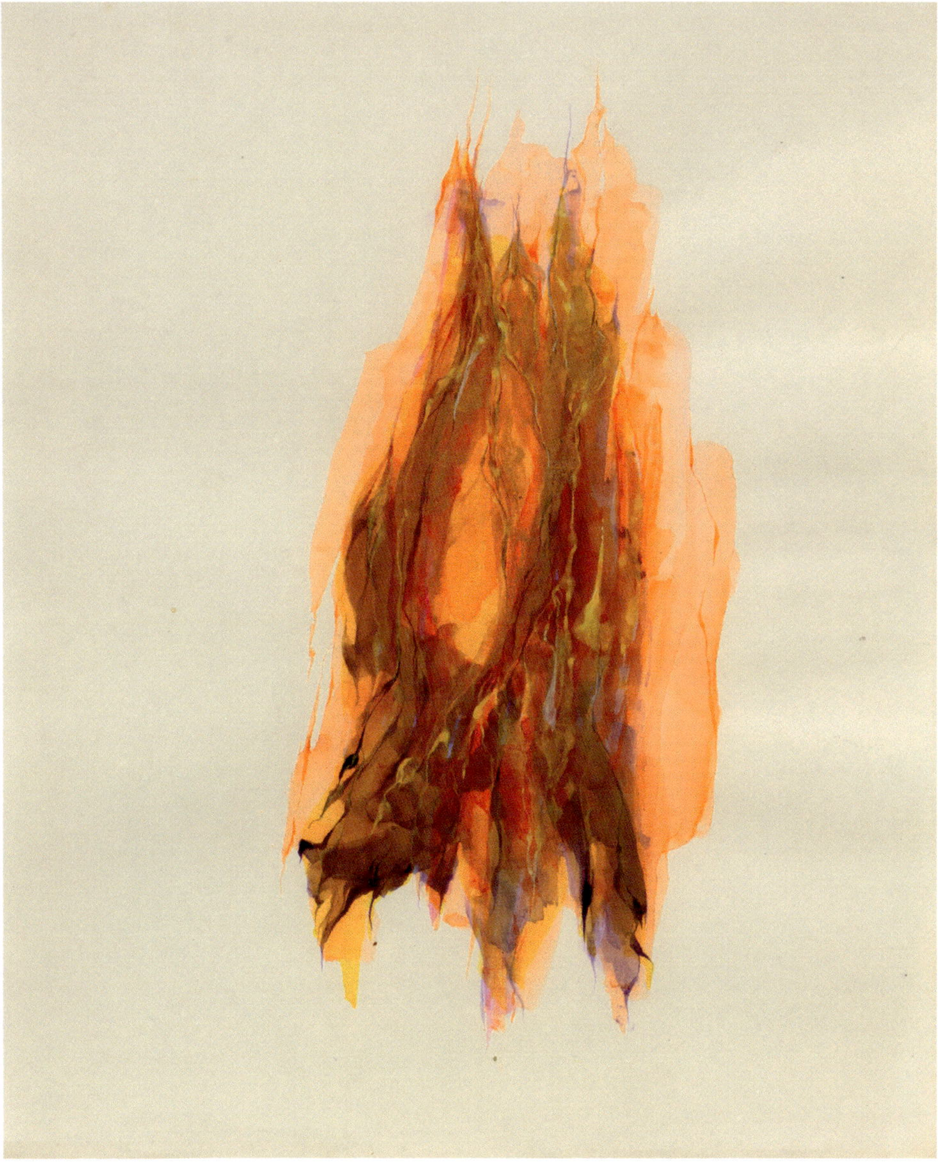

PL. 47 Cameron, *Untitled* (from the *Lion Path* series), n.d.

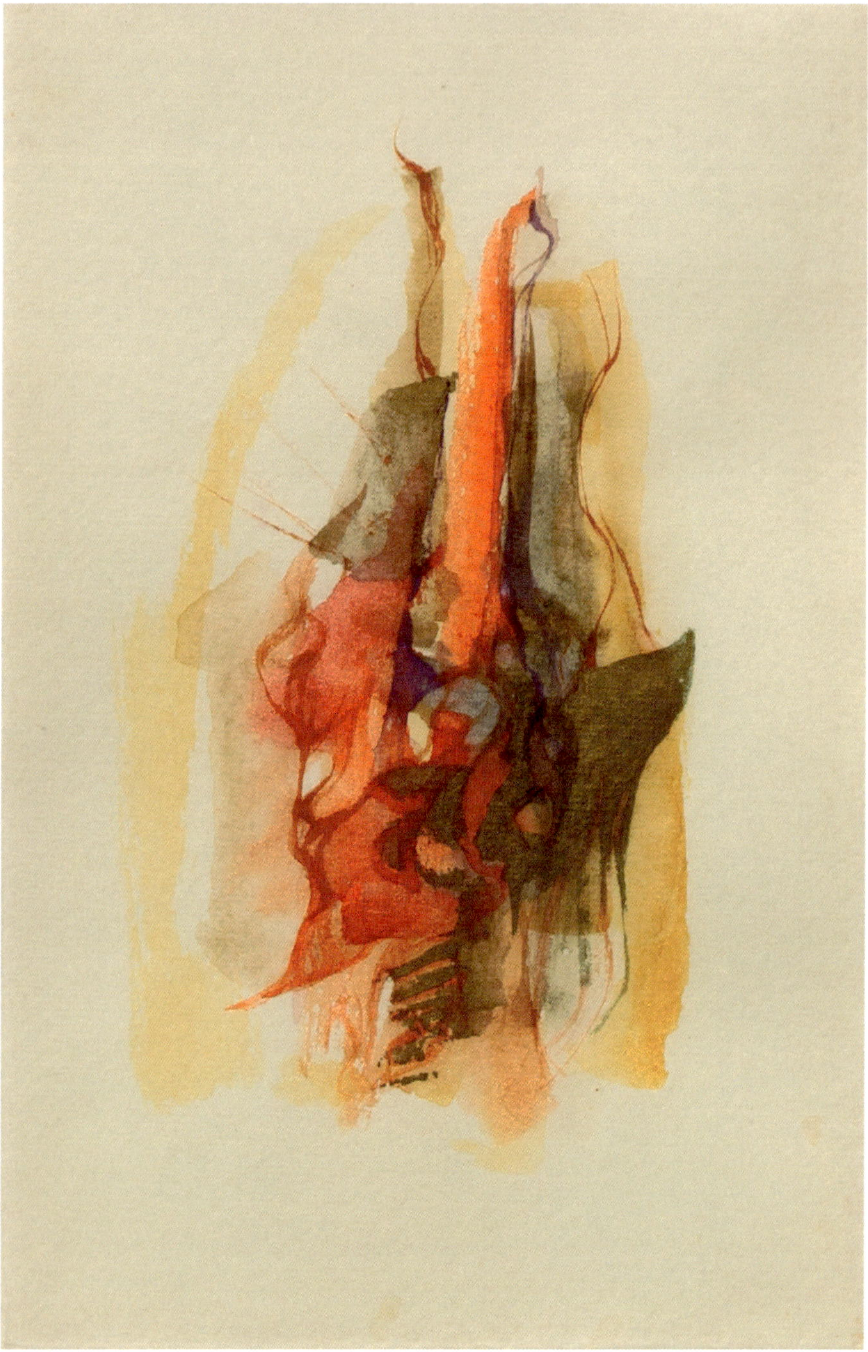

PL. 48 Cameron, *Untitled* (from the *Lion Path* series), n.d.

PL. 49 Elizabeth Milleker, *Portal*, 2010

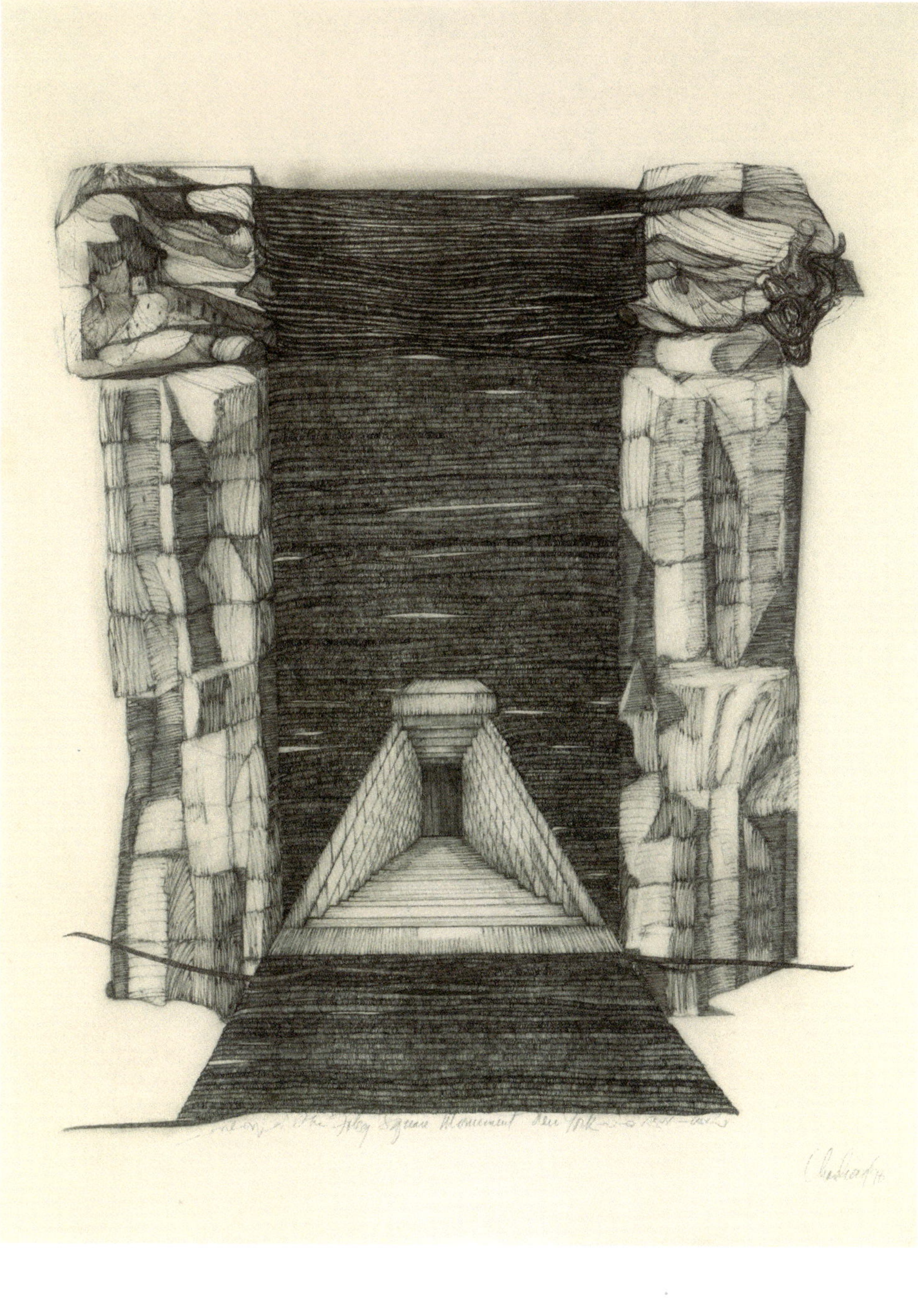

PL. 50 Barbara Chase-Riboud, *The Foley Square Monument New York*, from the *Monument Drawings* series, 1996

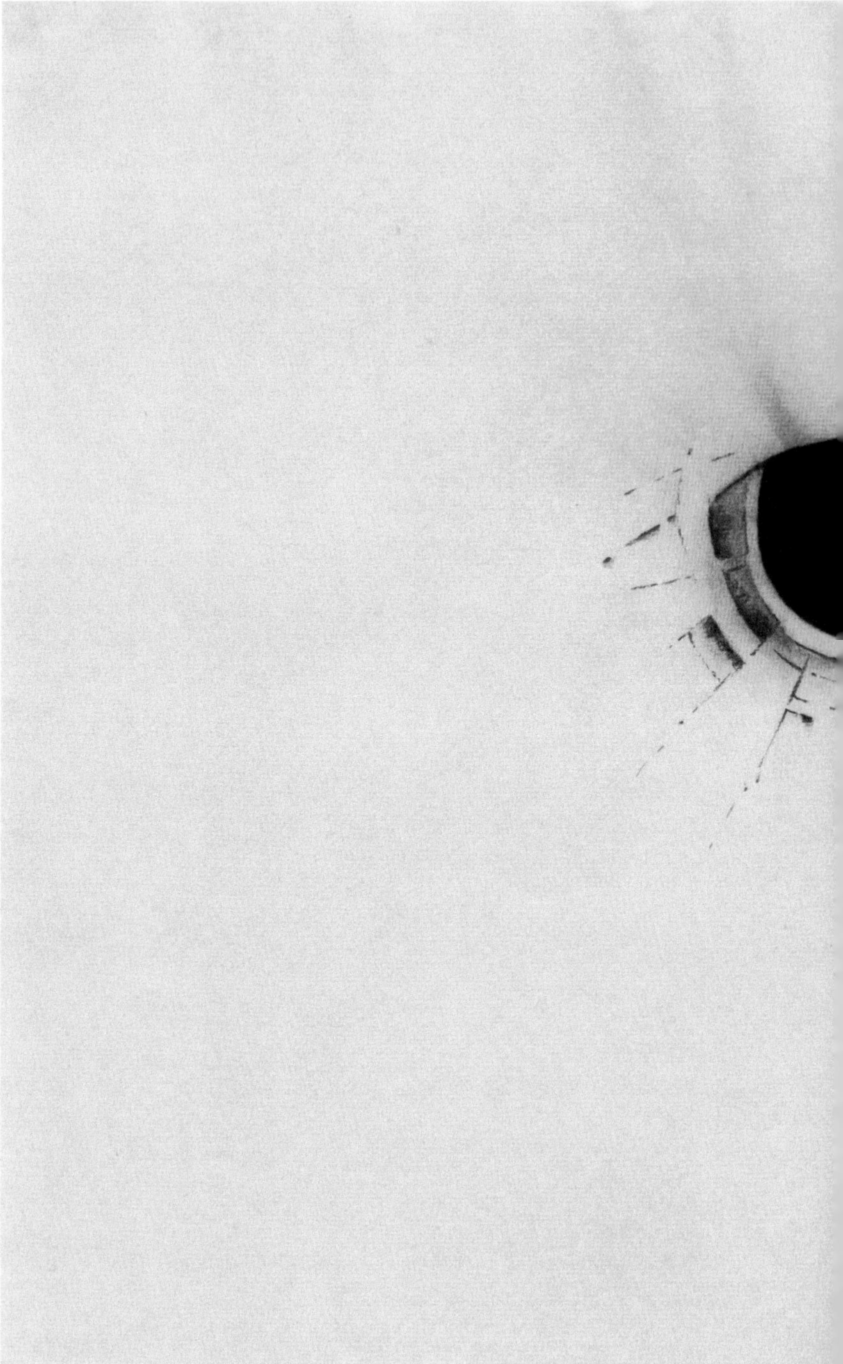

PL. 51 Lee Bontecou, *Untitled*, 1960

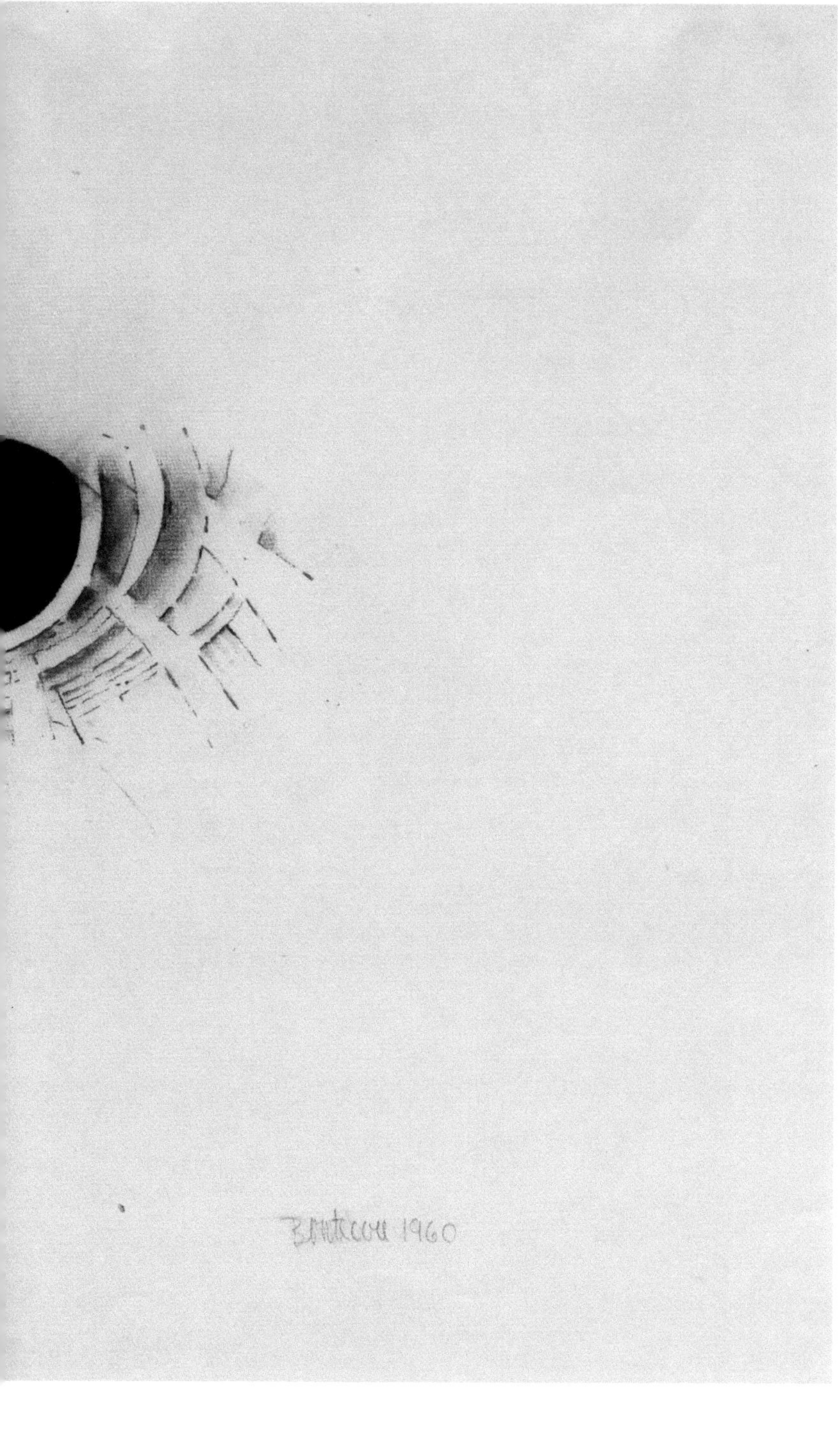
Bontecou 1960

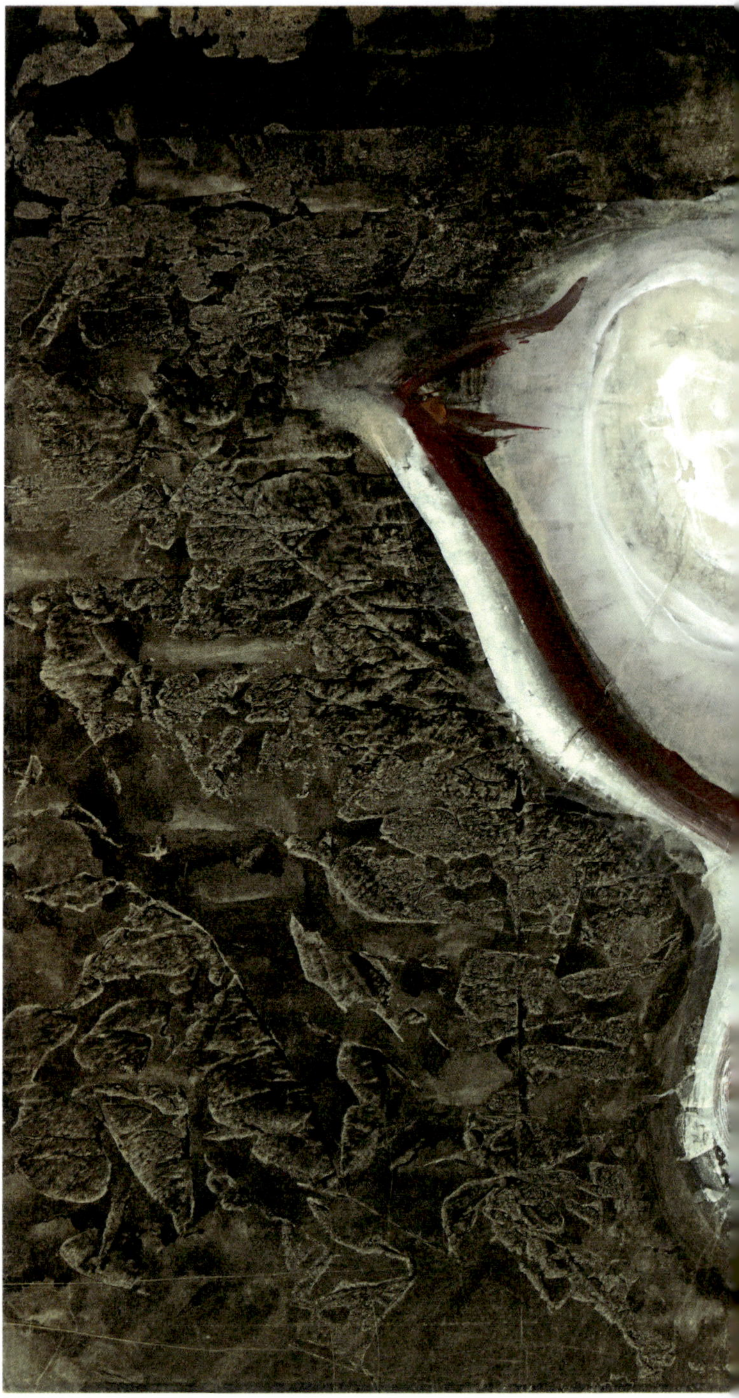

PL. 52 Morris Graves, *Chalice*, 1942

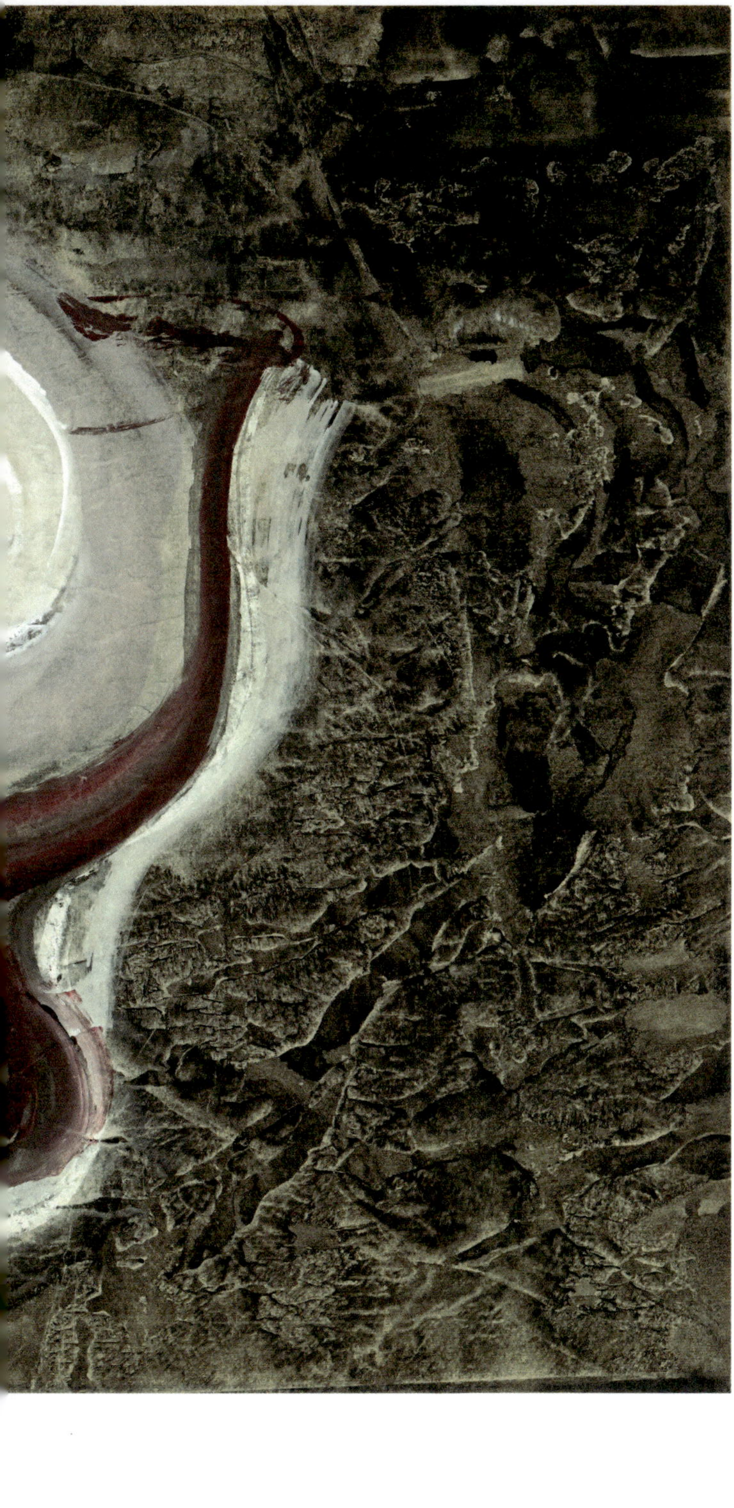

Works in the Exhibition

PL. 1
Mel Chin
Garden where the Wild Grass Obscures the True Pearl, 1987
Graphite on drawing paper laminated on plywood
13 x 13 inches (33 x 33 cm)
Courtesy of Amanda Wiles

PL. 2
Mel Chin
Tantric Dream Diagram, 1991
Pigment and paper on roofing slate
14 1/4 x 8 inches (36.2 x 20.3 cm)
Courtesy of the artist

PL. 3
Jordan Belson
Peacock Book Drawing 07, 1952
Ink on paper
13 x 5 3/4 inches (33 x 14.6 cm)
Estate of Jordan Belson, Courtesy of Matthew Marks Gallery

PL. 4
Roland Barthes
Sans titre-22 octobre 1973, 1973
Ink on paper
10 3/8 x 13 3/4 inches (26.3 x 35.1 cm)
Centre Pompidou, Paris, National Museum of Modern Art-Industrial Design Centre

PL. 5
Roland Barthes
Sans titre-31 mars 1974, 1974
Color pencil and marker on paper
8 1/8 x 10 1/2 inches (20.8 x 26.8 cm)
Centre Pompidou, Paris, National Museum of Modern Art-Industrial Design Centre

PL. 6
Robert Bittenbender
Saturina, 2018
Pastel and pencil on paper
13 1/2 x 15 1/2 inches (34.3 x 39.4 cm)
Collection of Matt Keegan, Courtesy of the artist

PL. 7
Ilka Gedő
Untitled (table #2), 1949
Charcoal and graphite on paper
31 x 41 inches (78.7 x 104.1 cm)
Courtesy of Shepherd Gallery

PL. 8
Georgia O'Keeffe
Untitled (Abstraction), 1970s
Graphite on paper
5 7/8 x 7 7/8 inches (14.9 x 20 cm)
Georgia O'Keeffe Museum, Gift of The Georgia O'Keeffe Foundation

PL. 9
Georgia O'Keeffe
Untitled (Abstraction), 1970s
Graphite on paper
5 7/8 x 7 7/8 inches (14.9 x 20 cm)
Georgia O'Keeffe Museum, Gift of The Georgia O'Keeffe Foundation

PL. 10
Georgia O'Keeffe
Untitled (Landscape), 1960s
Graphite on paper
6 1/2 x 8 3/4 inches (16.5 x 22.2 cm)
Georgia O'Keeffe Museum, Gift of The Georgia O'Keeffe Foundation

PL. 11
Hu Zhengyan
Illustration from the *Ten Bamboo Studio Manual of Calligraphy and Painting* (*Shizhuzhai shuhua pu*), 1679-1870
Ink printed on paper
9 7/8 x 11 inches (25 x 29 cm)
Loaned by the University of Pennsylvania Museum of Archaeology and Anthropology, Philadelphia, U.S.A.

PL. 12
Walter De Maria
Floating Mountain, c. 1961-64
Color pencil on paper
14 x 17 inches (35.6 x 43.2 cm)
© The Estate of Walter De Maria, Courtesy Gagosian

PL. 13
Duane Linklater
break up swept up all of the willows 1, 2022
Cochineal, sumac, acrylic paint, medium on paper
30 x 22 inches (76 x 57 cm)
Courtesy of the artist and Catriona Jeffries, Vancouver

PL. 14
Elizabeth Milleker
Underworld of the Brain, 2010
Watercolor
7 x 11 inches (17.8 x 27.9 cm)
Courtesy of the artist

PL. 15
Duane Linklater
Migraine 2, 2022
Graphite on paper
12 x 9 inches (31 x 23 cm)
Courtesy of the artist and Catriona Jeffries, Vancouver

PL. 16
Duane Linklater
Migraine 1, 2022
Graphite on paper
12 x 9 inches (31 x 23 cm)
Courtesy of the artist and Catriona Jeffries, Vancouver

PL. 17
Duane Linklater
Migraine 3, 2022
Graphite on paper
15 x 11 inches (38 x 28 cm)
Courtesy of the artist and Catriona Jeffries, Vancouver

PL. 18
Jordan Belson
Brain Drawing, 1952
Ink on paper
7 11/16 x 7 5/16 (19.5 x 20 cm)
Estate of Jordan Belson, Courtesy of Matthew Marks Gallery

PL. 19
Jordan Belson
Brain Drawing, 1952
Ink on paper
7 13/16 x 7 13/16 inches (19.8 x 19.8 cm)
Estate of Jordan Belson, Courtesy of Matthew Marks Gallery

PL. 20
Unknown Shaker artist
Word of the Saviour, 1843
Ink on paper
16 5/16 x 32 3/16 inches (41.4 x 81.6 cm)
Shaker Museum, Chatham and New Lebanon, New York

PL. 21
Bernadette Van-Huy
Home Improvements, 2019
UV print on plexi
18 x 24 inches (45.7 x 61 cm)
Courtesy of the artist

PL. 22
Bernadette Van-Huy
Spinning with Spinoza, 2019
UV print on plexi
18 x 24 inches (45.7 x 61 cm)
Courtesy of Thea Westreich Wagner & Ethan Wagner

PL. 23, COVER
Julia Phillips
Dance Marks, 2014
Monotype
33 7/8 × 33 7/8 inches (86 × 86 cm)
Courtesy of the artist and Matthew Marks Gallery, New York

PL. 24
Betye Saar
Taurus, 1967
Intaglio print, ink, and watercolor on paper
13 1/2 x 21 1/2 inches (34.3 x 54.6 cm)
Courtesy of Ortuzar Projects

PL. 25
Janet Malcolm
Ermine (from the *Emily Dickinson Series*), 2013
Paper collage
9 x 14 3/4 inches (22.9 x 37.5 cm)
Private collection,
Courtesy of Bookstein Projects

PL. 26
Janet Malcolm
Cleopatra (from the *Emily Dickinson Series*), 2013
Paper collage
14 x 21 inches (35.6 x 53.3 cm)
Private collection,
Courtesy of Bookstein Projects

PL. 27
Mel Chin
Study for Mercury: The Principle of Polarity–The Orbital Rebus, 1987
Ink and graphite on vellum
23 3/4 x 35 5/8 inches (60.3 x 90.5 cm)
Courtesy of the artist

PL. 28
Jack Whitten
Radiator Drawing #5, 2010
Graphite on rice paper
19 1/2 x 27 inches (49.5 x 68.6 cm)
Jack Whitten Estate

PL. 29
Cameron
Pluto Transiting the Twelfth House, 1978-86
Ink on paper
12 x 9 inches (30.5 x 22.9 cm)
Courtesy Nicole Klagsbrun and The Cameron Parsons Foundation

PL. 30
Lenore Tawney
Eclipse, 1965
Ink on paper
9 1/2 x 9 1/2 inches (24 x 24 cm)
Courtesy of the Lenore G. Tawney Foundation, New York, and Alison Jacques, London

PL. 31
Lenore Tawney
Untitled, 1965
India ink on graph paper
11 3/8 x 18 inches (29 x 45.6 cm)
Courtesy of the Lenore G. Tawney Foundation, New York, and Alison Jacques, London

PL. 32
Yutaka Matsuzawa
Untitled, 1960-63
Offset lithograph with ink drawing
8 13/16 x 8 7/8 inches (22.4 x 22.5 cm)
Museum of Modern Art, Art & Project/ Depot VBVR Gift, 2007

PL. 33
Unknown artist, Rajasthan
Sarvatobhadra Yantra, c. 18th-19th century
Gouache on paper
18 1/4 x 16 3/4 inches (46.4 x 42.5 cm)
Courtesy of Joost van den Bergh, London

PL. 34
Cici Wu
The Disappearance of Yu Man-hon (storyboard 02), 2017
Mineral pigments, glue, and Japanese paper
42 x 26 inches (106.7 x 66 cm)
Courtesy of Olivia Rubell

PL. 35
Yutaka Matsuzawa
Untitled, 1960-63
Cut and pasted paper on color paper
13 3/8 × 9 7/16 inches (33.9 × 24 cm)
Museum of Modern Art, Art & Project/ Depot VBVR Gift, 2007

PL. 36
Jo Baer
Untitled, 1960
Pencil and color pencil on paper
9 x 7 inches (22.9 x 17.8 cm)
Courtesy of the artist and Pace Gallery

PL. 37
Jo Baer
Untitled, 1960
Pencil on paper
4 1/8 x 4 13/16 inches (10.5 x 12.2 cm)
Courtesy of the artist and Pace Gallery

PL. 38
Jo Baer
Untitled, 1960
Pencil on paper
4 1/2 x 6 inches (11.4 x 15.2 cm)
Courtesy of the artist and Pace Gallery

PL. 39
Warlimpirrnga Tjapaltjarri
Maruwa, 2017
Acrylic on Belgian linen
74 x 60 1/4 inches (188.1 x 153 cm)
Collection of Steve Martin and
Anne Stringfield

PL. 40
Mohammed O. Khalil
Bomb Cantata, 1968
Etching and surface roll
on copper plate printed
with intaglio ink on paper
19 5/8 x 15 3/4 inches (50 x 40 cm)
Courtesy of the artist

PL. 41
I. Rice Pereira
Untitled, 1934
Ink on paper
9 x 11 inches (22.9 x 27.9 cm)
Courtesy of Anita Shapolsky Gallery

PL. 42
Mohammed O. Khalil
The Second Queen, 1974
Marbling and scraping
on copper plate printed with
intaglio ink on paper
17 1/2 x 14 1/2 inches (44.5 x 36.8 cm)
Courtesy of the artist

PL. 43
Arnold J. Kemp
Index, 2021
Ink on handmade woven paper
23 3/8 x 19 inches (59.4 x 48.3 cm)
Courtesy of the artist and Martos Gallery

PL. 44
Steffani Jemison
Black Utopia (Sol), 2017
UV inkjet on mirrored acrylic
59 x 59 inches (149.9 x 149.9 cm)
Carmel Barasch Family Collection

PL. 45
Yutaka Matsuzawa
Untitled, 1960-63
Oil on board
12 x 11 7/8 inches (30.5 x 30 cm)
Collection of Matsuzawa Kumiko

PL. 46
Cameron
Untitled (from the *Lion Path* series), n.d.
Watercolor on paper
14 x 11 inches (35.6 x 27.9 cm)
Courtesy of Nicole Klagsbrun and
The Cameron Parsons Foundation

PL. 47
Cameron
Untitled (from the *Lion Path* series), n.d.
Mixed media on paper
17 x 14 inches (43.2 x 35.6 cm)
Courtesy of Nicole Klagsbrun and
The Cameron Parsons Foundation

PL. 48
Cameron
Untitled (from the *Lion Path* series), n.d.
Watercolor on envelope
7 1/4 x 4 3/4 inches (18.4 x 12.1 cm)
Courtesy Nicole Klagsbrun and
The Cameron Parsons Foundation

PL. 49
Elizabeth Milleker
Portal, 2010
Watercolor
7 1/2 x 10 inches (19.1 x 25.4 cm)
Courtesy of the artist

PL. 50
Barbara Chase-Riboud
The Foley Square Monument New York, from the *Monument Drawings* series, 1996
Charcoal, charcoal pencil, and ink over etching and aquatint
31 1/2 x 24 inches (80 x 61 cm)
Yale University Art Gallery,
Janet and Simeon Braguin Fund

PL. 51
Lee Bontecou
Untitled, 1960
Charcoal and pencil on paper
19 x 25 1/8 inches (48.3 x 63.8 cm)
Museum of Modern Art,
Gift of James L. Goodwin in memory of Philip L. Goodwin, 1962

PL. 52
Morris Graves
Chalice, 1942
Tempera and ink on paper mounted on paperboard
25 3/4 x 29 3/4 inches (65.4 x 75.6 cm)
Collection of halley k harrisburg and Michael Rosenfeld, New York

NOT PICTURED
Andrei Tarkovsky,
Compiled by Clay Hapaz
Film clips of the Ocean Consciousness in *Solaris,* 1972
Compilation of film clips
1912 x 806 px; 3:33 min.
Courtesy of Clay Hapaz

Image Credits

FIG. 1 Courtesy Bookstein Projects, New York, Photo by Etienne Frossard, New York
PL. 1 Courtesy of the artist
PLS. 4, 5 © Michel Salzedo
PL. 7 Photo by Daniel Terna
PL. 8, 9, 10 © 2022 Georgia O'Keeffe Museum / Artists Rights Society (ARS), New York
PL. 12 Courtesy of Gagosian, Photo by Rob McKeever
PLS. 13, 15, 16, 17 Courtesy Catriona Jeffries, Vancouver, Photo by Rachel Topham Photography
PLS. 14, 49 Photo by Joseph Coscia Jr.
PL. 23 © Julia Phillips, Courtesy Matthew Marks Gallery
PL. 24 Courtesy the artist and Ortuzar Projects, New York, Photo by Timothy Doyon
PLS. 25, 26 Courtesy of the Estate of the Artist and Bookstein Projects, New York, Photo by Etienne Frossard, New York
PL. 28 © Jack Whitten Estate
PLS. 29, 46–48 Photo by Daniel Terna
PL. 30, 31 © Lenore G. Tawney Foundation, Photo by Michael Brzezinski
PL. 33 Photo by Matt Pia, London
PLS. 32, 35 © 2022 Yutaka Matsuzawa
PL. 39 © Copyright Agency, Licensed by Artists Rights Society (ARS), New York, 2022, Photo by Bruce M. White
PL. 43 Photo by Charles Benton
PL. 44 Courtesy of the artist and Greene Naftali, New York, Photo by Zeshan Ahmed
PL. 45 © 2022 Yutaka Matsuzawa, Courtesy of the Collection of Matsuzawa Kumiko and Empty Gallery
PL. 50 © Barbara Chase-Riboud, Courtesy of Lucia Momoh/Jeffrey Johnston
PL. 51 © 2022 Lee Bontecou
PL. 52 © Morris Graves Foundation, Courtesy of Michael Rosenfeld Gallery LLC

Contributors

Elise Duryee-Browner is an artist and writer living in New York. She studied International Relations at Wellesley College. She has had recent solo shows at Graham Vunderink Gallery in Pittsfield, MA, and at Gandt in Astoria, NY. She has written essays for *May Revue* and *Texte zur Kunst* in addition to several press releases and monograph texts. She is in the process of writing a book.

E. C. Feiss is a writer and postdoc in the History of Art department at the Ohio State University. Her work has recently appeared in *American Art* and in an essay for *Blank Forms*.

Maya Hayda is a curator, writer, and art historian based in New York. She has worked with Artists Space and Canal Projects and written for *Public Parking*. Her research interests are rooted in questions of materiality, analogy, and the confluences of natural and built environments, examining art as an interdisciplinary framework which exposes and engages relations between people, objects, conditions, and broader ecologies. She is a graduate of Wesleyan University with a degree in Art History and English.

Annie Ochmanek is a Ph.D. candidate in art history at Columbia University. Her writings have appeared in *Artforum*, Texte zur Kunst, and exhibition catalogs for The Museum of Modern Art, New York; the Albright-Knox Art Gallery, Buffalo; and Z33 Hasselt, Belgium. A former Curatorial Assistant at MoMA and former Associate Editor of *Artforum*, she is co-editor of the recent *October Files* volume on Donald Judd (The MIT Press).

Lauren O'Neill-Butler is a writer whose book *Let's Have a Talk: Conversations with Women on Art and Culture* (Karma, 2021) brings together nearly ninety interviews. A cofounder of the nonprofit magazine *November* and a former Senior Editor of *Artforum* magazine, she has also contributed to *Aperture*, *Art Journal*, *Bookforum*, and *The New York Times*. In 2020, she received a Warhol Foundation Art Writers Grant.

Olivia Shao is a curator based in New York. She has organized exhibitions and projects at independent spaces, galleries, and institutions in New York City and Los Angeles as well as in Europe and Asia.

Published on the occasion of the exhibition *Of Mythic Worlds: Works from the Distant Past through the Present*

Organized by Olivia Shao

The Drawing Center
March 8–May 14, 2023

Lead support for *Of Mythic Worlds: Works from the Distant Past through the Present* is provided by the Burger Collection, Hong Kong and the TOY family, along with The Andy Warhol Foundation for the Visual Arts. Generous funding is provided by the ADAA Foundation, the Fundación Almine y Bernard Ruiz-Picasso para el Arte, Lonti Ebers, and Gagosian. Additional support is provided by the Director's Circle of The Drawing Center.

This is number 151 of the Drawing Papers, a series of publications documenting The Drawing Center's exhibitions and programs and providing a forum for the study of drawing.

Editor
Joanna Ahlberg

Design
Dandelion / Peter Ahlberg

Printing & Binding
Shapco Printing, Minneapolis, MN

About the Type
This book is set in Publico Text (Roman, Italic, and Bold). It is part of the Publico Collection, designed by Ross Milne, Christian Schwartz, Paul Barnes, Kai Bernau, and Greg Gazdowicz, and released incrementally by Commercial Type in 2009, 2013, and 2014. This book also uses Plain (Regular and Italic), which was designed by François Rappo and released by Optimo Type Foundry in 2014.

ISBN 979-8-9876009-0-0

THE
DRAWING
CENTER